RENEWALS: 691-4574

DATE DUE

NOV 0 1			
NOV 2 3			

Foreign
Exchange
Today

To
Mary, Jonathan, Fiona and Jeremy

Foreign Exchange Today

RAYMOND G. F. CONINX
Vice President, The First National Bank of Chicago

A HALSTED PRESS BOOK

JOHN WILEY & SONS
New York

Published in the USA
by Halsted Press, a Division
of John Wiley & Sons, Inc.
New York

© Raymond G. F. Coninx 1978

Library of Congress Cataloging in Publication Data

Coninx, Raymond G   F
Foreign exchange today

"A Halsted Press book"
Bibliography: p.
1. Foreign Exchange. 1. Title
HG3821-C77 1977   332.4'5   77-11932
ISBN 0-470-99315-4

The views expressed in this book are those of the author and are not
necessarily representative of those of The First National Bank of
Chicago.

Printed in Great Britain by
Billings Ltd, Guildford, Surrey

Preface

Over the years the thought of writing an introduction to foreign exchange crossed my mind on a number of occasions. I postponed the decision to put my ideas on paper time and time again, as interest in the subject seemed to be limited to professional foreign exchange dealers, treasurers of multi-national corporations and a few academics. The fact that Paul Einzig had covered the theory of the foreign exchanges in numerous works also provided me with a ready excuse for not trying to improve on perfection.

The advent of floating exchange rates a few years ago, and the frequent and continuing currency crises, have, however, given me the incentive to marshal my thoughts on the subject. The knowledge that foreign exchange has become of vital concern to all organizations involved in international finance is, to say the least, a great encouragement. Even experts who, in the past, would have busied themselves with more esoteric financial matters have taken up the study of foreign exchange.

As with any topic of current interest, books and articles appear almost daily analysing particular aspects of the currency markets and their impact on business decisions. Earnest endeavours are being made to find a universally applicable solution to the problems which currency exposures create for treasurers and accountants. Suggestions abound: cash management programmes with or without netting, 'off the peg' or 'tailor-made' forecasting models, accounting methods, and many others. The wealth of financial wisdom which is being offered to the commercial practitioner must leave him in a state of shock, and often no wiser than he was before. This is not surprising as it seems unlikely that there will be two companies with the same *modus operandi*, range of products, capital base or business environment. As a result the excellent advice offered cannot be put into practice because it does not fit the specific situation.

Only the main risk-takers, the commercial companies and their executives, are in a position to decide which foreign exchange techniques are appropriate for their particular overall strategy. In *Foreign Exchange Today* I intend to give the commercial user an outline of current foreign exchange practices and some indication of how the professional dealers in the banks think, and put their thinking into practice. It would be foolish to suggest that all dealers act or react in the same way, but usually there is a degree of consensus which may not be apparent at the time. This background knowledge may help the 'outsider' to understand foreign exchange movements that at first sight seem opposed to common sense.

Chapters 1 to 6 of the book deal with the origins and recent history of the foreign exchange markets, important theoretical definitions and the factors which influence foreign exchange rates. Chapters 7 to 12 concentrate on the practical aspects of foreign exchange techniques, accounting procedures and foreign exchange rate forecasting.

I would like to emphasize again that it was never my intention to construct a set of solutions covering every eventuality. Nevertheless, I hope that after reading this book the 'foreign language' of the trade will seem less forbidding than before. I have in fact deliberately avoided the use of some contemporary jargon, which confounds even the professionals.

As current exchange rates date very quickly, fictional rates bearing some resemblance to identifiable currencies have been employed in the theoretical examples (*see* Appendix A, p. 150).

In the process of simplifying a subject as complex as foreign exchange, I have had to exclude some, to my mind, superfluous events, theories and practices which other observers may believe to be of prime importance. For this I apologize.

October 1977   R.G.F.C.

Contents

7

Page

1. The origins of foreign exchange

Unless they are connected with international business in their daily lives, the privileged inhabitants of the developed world come into contact with the foreign exchange phenomenon only when they go abroad for a change of scenery. 'Foreign exchange' for holiday-makers is embodied in the bank-notes of other countries, which somehow never look quite as respectable as their own national issue. If they are security-conscious they may even purchase travellers' cheques. Some travellers become adept currency dealers when they wake up to the fact that the conversion rates offered for their notes or cheques differ from place to place. They find that modest savings can be made by shopping around for the best rate. These minor discrepancies in the quoted rates may not spoil the fun of the sun-seeker, but they can make an international business deal a profitable venture or just a waste of time.

Foreign exchange and foreign exchange rates

It may be appropriate first to define our subject for readers who are not familiar with the theory of economics and foreign exchange. Foreign exchange is the act of converting the currency of one country into the currency of another. To execute this seemingly simple transaction a price or value is fixed for the currency which is being acquired or bought and this price is called the *foreign exchange rate*.

Foreign exchange transactions, entered into to settle international trade or financial operations, are rarely finalized in bank-notes. It would be cumbersome and also very risky to carry suitcases full of notes from one country to another (though in recent years intrepid voyagers have smuggled large sums in bank-notes across mountain passes in order to convert them into a more stable currency on the other side). We shall investigate the practicalities of currency settlements in Chapter 7—suffice it to mention here that exchange transactions are usually settled by transfers, from one account to another, in a foreign centre. This procedure is very similar to the one applied when money is transferred from one town to another within a country, for instance from Liverpool to London or from New York to San Francisco.

The demand, or lack of it, will decide the price or exchange rate for a currency. This practice is no different from that which operates in other markets. The greengrocer who goes to the early morning market will have to pay more for his fruit or vegetables if they are in short supply; similarly, a currency cheapens or gets dearer according to its availability or dearth. With some qualification, it could be said that money is just another commodity.

Direct and indirect quotations

In most of the world's money centres, exchange rates are quoted in terms of the national currency. For example, in New York the pound sterling will be quoted as being worth US $1.70 or US $2.00, or whatever the value of sterling is at the time. In other words, one pound equals 1.70 dollars, or whatever.

One of the vestiges of the time when sterling was of world-wide importance is the *indirect quotation system* of the London market, which values one pound in whole or part units of foreign currencies. Thus London quotes the value of sterling instead of the value of the foreign currency. This approach does not create problems for the experienced dealer, but it does mean that the casual user of the market has to divide a foreign currency amount by the exchange rate to find the sterling equivalent rather than using the simpler multiplication method of the *direct quotation system*.

With the rapid communications available to operators in the foreign exchange markets, the rates in different money centres will practically always be in equilibrium. The minor distortions which may show up from one centre to another, or for that matter one bank to another, will reflect the natural supply or demand situation, but usually they are of little consequence.

In principle, market forces will bring all rates to an equilibrium.

For instance, if one Deutsche Mark is worth 40 cents in New York, one dollar will be valued at DM 2.50 in Frankfurt, for one dollar divided by 40 cents equals 2.50. If local demand in New York, during the time that Europe and the United States can operate together, resulted in an appreciation of the Deutsche Mark to 41 cents, this would immediately be reflected in Frankfurt. Otherwise, smart operators would contact Germany to sell dollars at DM 2.50, and immediately sell the Deutsche Marks in New York, making a handsome profit in the process.

Some foreign exchange dealers make it their business to take advantage of such minor discrepancies. This activity is called *arbitrage*, and involves the buying and selling of a currency in different centres.

This brief description of the foreign exchange markets is but a glimpse of the complexities which beset the currency world, but on it all further discussion is based.

Bimetallism and the Gold Standards

Foreign exchange is not a new-fangled idea; it has existed in various guises since time immemorial. But in its current application it has really only existed since the end of the First World War. Before the First World War the external values of currencies were mainly determined by their worth as expressed in gold or silver. Furthermore, this worth was realizable only if there was no restriction placed on the convertibility of the national note issue into either of these precious metals.

Traditionally, a currency was considered to be fully convertible if notes and coinage could be freely exchanged for gold at the central bank's counters, but convertibility into gold ceased to be practicable after the First World War. The contemporary definition of a *convertible currency* would be one that can be used to purchase other currencies without let or hindrance from the monetary authorities. Some currencies when in the hands of non-residents can be fully convertible, while residents of the country are prohibited by regulations from acquiring foreign currencies. These currencies would then be said to have *limited convertibility* only.

Under a bimetallic standard it was normal for countries to set gold to silver ratios. This ratio was intended to stop speculative movements from silver to gold and vice versa. Also it was useful for the general public to know that one gold coin equalled a certain number of silver ones; it was thus unnecessary for the individual to acquire the skills of an assayer. At the outset, the set ratios may have reflected the current availability balance between silver and gold, but the vagaries of mining and refining very rapidly produced imbalances. A gold discovery in the New World, or increased silver production, could tip the scales in favour of one or the other. Whenever a fundamental disequilibrium showed up, the cognoscenti of the time would hoard the coins struck in the more valuable metal, and before very long they disappeared completely from circulation.

The maxim attributed to Sir Thomas Gresham—Gresham's Law—very aptly describes a metal supply imbalance: 'Bad money drives out good.' This saying is still as valid today as it was in the sixteenth century; Sir Thomas was referring not just to supply imbalances but also to the fact that some rulers would deliberately debase the coinage struck by decreasing its precious metal content.

In spite of the spirited defence put up by its supporters, the bimetallic standard eventually gave way to the one-metal standard, or *monometallism*. By the beginning of the twentieth century countries like Great Britain and the United States had implemented the 'Full' or 'Specie Gold Standard' and this Gold Standard ruled supreme for several decades domestically and internationally. Countries with no access to mined gold, or too poor to take part in the extravaganza, adopted the Gold Exchange Standard. The countries on the Gold Exchange Standard simply kept the bulk of their foreign reserves in the currencies of countries which followed the 'Full Gold Standard'. The knowledge that the pound sterling and the dollar were literally worth their weight in gold allayed any fears about the absence of gold in their coffers. Any time a Gold Exchange Standard country needed the yellow metal badly it sold part of its hard currency holdings for gold. It then gained the additional benefit that surplus reserves could be invested in Treasury Bills or other suitable paper and earn interest, instead of incurring a safekeeping charge for bullion lying in some dank vault.

It is doubtful whether gold could ever again play a leading role in the international payment system. It had its uses for a number of decades; it seemed to encourage monetary discipline until the First World War. But for practical purposes, for gold to keep pace with the expansion of the world's economies, it would have to be either mined in greater quantities or regularly upvalued, and neither prospect is very likely. In any case, to dig a hole in one place and put the extracted contents in another hole—or vault— is not a particularly productive activity, unless you happen to own a gold mine.

After the First World War most countries abandoned the Full Gold Standard by default: there was not enough gold around to back the inflated note circulations of the war-damaged economies. Most countries then adopted the Gold Exchange Standard, or a version of it. Some relied largely on gold but others preferred to keep the bulk of their reserves in countries which still settled official claims in gold. The term *hard currency* which before 1939 would have referred to a currency backed by large gold holdings now describes one with large foreign currency reserves.

In 1925 Great Britain tried to reintroduce an amended Gold Standard, the Gold Bullion Standard, but had to give up the attempt in 1931. The Gold Bullion Standard has been blamed for the General Strike of 1926 and the stagnation of the British economy during the years 1925–1931. Possibly it was not so much that gold had been reinstated but rather that the sterling price was too low and thus could not be sustained against speculative pressures from abroad.

The lesson that should have been learned from the British experiment was that national pride is not a rational basis for the fixing of a gold price or an exchange rate level. However, other countries and their governments consider their currencies equally sacrosanct.

In spite of the Gold Exchange Standard, the inter-war years were marred by a number of competitive devaluations—at least they were interpreted by others to have been made for competitive reasons. To ensure that there would be peace on the economic front after the war was over, the nations of the free world met at Bretton Woods in 1944 while it was still being fought to try to put the international monetary system to rights.

2. From Bretton Woods to the 1967 sterling devaluation

It is often said that experience cannot be taught. Though we may agree wholeheartedly with this statement, it is also true that even second-hand experience is better than none. Very few of today's Stock Exchange members lived and worked through the Great Crash of 1929, but one would hope that they have read about it and assimilated the underlying causes of this, in retrospect, salutary occurrence.

Unfortunately, apprentice foreign exchange dealers do not as a rule undergo a period of formal training in their profession. Usually, they are chosen because they show aptitude in dealing. Whatever knowledge they gain afterwards is passed on to them verbally in a piecemeal fashion. Experience is obtained through repeatedly making mistakes, hopefully only minor ones which do not cost the bank a fortune. This hit-and-miss method of training dealers is then supposed to produce top-quality money experts. No wonder only a few make the grade. Foreign exchange executives in commercial companies are usually much better qualified, but they do not have dealing experience and have only a limited knowledge of monetary history.

The professional dealer and the commercial operator both have much to gain by the study of economic and monetary history. They will find this background knowledge invaluable when they come across a situation which is a carbon copy of a past event. Their second-hand experience may not produce larger profits, but it may help to avoid substantial losses.

1944-1949

Until 1971, the decisions taken at Bretton Woods dominated the international monetary scene. The Bretton Woods Conference in 1944 was organized to establish an orderly international payments system after the end of hostilities. The agreement covered a whole range of practical rulings which would govern currency parities, devaluation procedures, subscriptions to the International Monetary Fund (IMF), borrowing quotas, and other considerations. Parities would be fixed against gold and thus indirectly against the US dollar as, at least for official settlements, the dollar was linked to gold. It is ironic to think now that some of the nations not in attendance have in actual fact performed better than those who were represented. That the new system relied primarily on the US dollar was not surprising as the United States, and to a lesser extent Canada, had become the repository of the free world's reserves.

The traditional advocates of the gold standard were again successful in imposing their views, and gold continued to be used as the numeraire for fixing the exchange rates for the various currencies.

There can be little doubt that grave mistakes were made at Bretton Woods which later came to bedevil the currency markets. However, the time was 1944. The end of the war was at last in sight and in the general euphoria it was readily assumed that economic and monetary peace would prevail internationally for the foreseeable future.

Some of the participants endowed with more realism, in particular the United Kingdom representative Lord Keynes, expressed their concern about the restoration of gold. Keynes even suggested the creation of a new international settlements vehicle to substitute for gold—'Bancor', a form of paper gold (one wonders whether he was secretly hopeful that the Gallic-sounding name might appeal to Britain's ally across the Channel). The *Special Drawing Rights* (SDRs) which were developed during the late 1960s and early 1970s were also based upon a Keynesian model.

Apart from worries about parities with gold, there was also the problem of the narrow upper and lower limits within which currencies were permitted to fluctuate: currencies could depreciate or appreciate only by 1 per cent either side of their parities. To make matters worse, many countries narrowed the band even further, to ¾ per cent either side of their parities, which meant that any significant demand or supply would necessitate the central banks defending the upper or lower support levels or intervention points. At these intervention points, a central bank, or the appropriate monetary agency in a country, was forced to buy or sell its own currency in the exchange markets to ensure that the rates did not move by more than the accepted margin from the parity. These support operations were essential to ensure that there were no *de facto* devaluations or revaluations, but in 1944 parity changes were not anticipated by most delegates. It was hoped that the members of the IMF, the operating arm of the international payments system, would exercise strict control over financial affairs so that currency re-alignments would be a thing of the past, and the exchange rate margins were deemed adequate to cope with seasonal fluctuations in demand and supply. The Gold Standard for official settlements, the narrow exchange rate bands and the rules which inhibited a flexible approach to exchange rate management all contributed to the eventual downfall of the Bretton Woods system.

Lord Keynes had been right to be concerned about future currency disequilibria, because trouble started very soon after the inauguration of the new system in 1946 and the establishment of the IMF in 1947. Unfortunately Keynes had died in 1946 and his wise counsel was greatly missed at the international conference tables.

By July 1947, Britain either had forgotten the lesson of the Gold Bullion Standard experiment in 1925, or was forced as a *quid pro quo* for a loan facility to change the foreign exchange regulations. Holders of transferable sterling were allowed to transfer funds to American sterling accounts; as these accounts carried the authorization for conversion into dollars, there was a substantial outflow of reserves. Only one month later, in August, the scheme had to be abrogated and sterling became once again inconvertible, unless one was a resident of the dollar area and granted the favour of an American sterling account.

The troubles which beset sterling during the 1950s and 1960s make excellent case studies for observers and interpreters of the currency markets. But the fate which befell sterling after the Second World War was only the prelude to more far-reaching dollar crises twenty-five years later.

Despite the cancellation of limited convertibility in 1947, sterling was in dire straits again by 1949. The British government had no option but to devalue the pound by a massive 30.5 per cent. The fact that a Labour government had to take this unpalatable decision may well have influenced later Conservative governments in their rigid stand against anything which smacked of devaluation —the political points which could be scored in elections by referring to Labour candidates as devaluers were too great to be ignored. In the 1960s the Labour government, which should have acted sooner, probably postponed the final decision to devalue until 1967 because it was well aware that it would be fashioning a weapon in the hands of its political opponents. It is, of course, preferable to take fiscal and economic measures when a currency is under pressure, but, once the exchange rate is out of control and reserves are being unnecessarily wasted, a drastic devaluation —by more than is actually required to redress the balance—is the only answer.

If in 1949 sterling had devalued in isolation, conditions might have been different during the 1950s and 1960s. As it happened, several major currencies joined in a chain reaction. Sweden and Holland devalued by approximately 30 per cent roughly in line with the United Kingdom, and even West Germany lowered the value of the Deutsche Mark by 20 per cent. Without a doubt the Germans' willingness to work was the mainspring of their 'economic miracle' in the late 1950s, but the post-war downward adjustment of the exchange rate, the 1949 devaluation, and Marshall Aid were in no small measure contributory factors. Most of the other currencies which devalued did not rank highly in the world financial stakes, but they made the British attempt to redress the balance less effective. It was not so much the concern about the United Kingdom's competitiveness in export markets which had inspired the other nations to take a devaluation route: it was a dread that internal inflationary pressures might cause a dollar drain. The constant anxiety that a dollar shortage would bring about a severe world liquidity crisis haunted international money men into the 1960s.

As the Bretton Woods parities were linked to gold, a devaluation was accomplished by raising the price of the precious metal in terms of the national currency, and conversely a revaluation required a decrease in its price. If other countries kept their gold parities unchanged, the devalued or revalued currency automatically adopted new exchange rates against all the rest. The terms 'devaluation' and 'revaluation' are usually applied in the context of gold-linked parities, although nowadays they are also used to describe a change in the value of a currency which has fixed parities against others. An exchange rate adjustment in a floating or free market would be referred to as a *depreciation* or *appreciation*. Devaluation and revaluation require deliberate actions; appreciation and depreciation normally reflect market activities.

With few exceptions—France, for instance—the 1949 devaluations fixed the parities of the major currencies for a dozen years.

1949-1961

The morbid preoccupation with the coming dollar shortage continued unabated even after the US balance of payments turned a solid red, even when American-produced goods became overpriced in the export markets, sometimes because import duties were prohibitive (or import licences unobtainable), and the only solution open to American industry was to move production lines overseas. The flow of US investments, especially into Europe, increased the balance of payments deficit further, as the positive effect of these investments, in the form of dividends, took a long time to materialize. Whether the investor took over an operating company or set up a new plant, the result was the same—an enormous outflow of dollars. And it was not only the loss of exports and the outflow of funds which gave cause for concern, but the fact that some products were cheaper to import than to produce in the United States.

Though it was less noticeable at the time, the US dollar had become over-valued. The reserve losses built up gradually but inexorably as the consequence of foreign aid programmes, uncompetitive export prices, overseas investments and rising imports. However, no remedial action was taken during the 1950s. The United Kingdom on the other hand, which had suffered more in the war, was economically in a worse position than the United States and there the over-valuation of the pound was felt almost immediately.

In 1949, the dollar still dominated the world, and continued to do so till the end of the 1950s. The United Kingdom, as part of the comprehensive foreign exchange regulations which applied at the time, even distinguished between the 'hard dollar' for investments in the dollar area and the 'soft dollar' for investments in other parts of the world.

As the hard dollar commanded a higher premium than the soft one, there were stringent reporting requirements to ensure that there was no overflow from the soft into the hard dollar pool.

The professional inter-bank exchange market in London, which had been closed down in 1939, was re-opened in 1952 and given a degree of freedom to encourage the gradual establishment of a market in London and with overseas banks. The government of the day was conservative with a small and large 'C' and believed in active markets and in economic and financial freedom.

Currency markets had continued to exist in centres unaffected by the war, but these were less than perfect. Supply and demand were rarely in balance and it was more a question of making long-term decisions and commitments as to future currency values. The normal market practices of quoting buying and selling rates were replaced by lengthy negotiations and thus there was no market in any real sense.

With the re-establishment of the foreign exchange markets in London and in Europe, though restricted by stringent foreign exchange regulations, the parities which had been fixed as a result of Bretton Woods and the 1949 revaluations now became subject to market pressures: supply and demand situations were open to scrutiny, interpretation and action by the market participants. With many more people and organizations involved in buying and selling, and with improved communications, information which previously had been the prerogative of a privileged few became available almost instantaneously to everyone.

Hemmed in by regulations, the markets could play only a limited role between 1952 and 1958. For instance, in the United Kingdom, the banks were not allowed to deal on *cross rates*. A cross rate is a rate which prices one foreign currency in terms of another, e.g. Deutsche Marks against US dollars in a third centre, for instance in London. The exception to this rule was the Canadian dollar against the US dollar, as they were considered of equal strength. Hence the rate for Canadian against US dollars is still referred to as the 'cross'. This restriction limited the ability of a dealer to cover opposite views taken in two currencies by executing one instead of two transactions. If a dealer had sold French francs and bought Deutsche Marks, both against sterling, and he wished to cancel the exposure, he was forced to buy back the francs against sterling and to sell the Deutsche Marks against sterling, two transactions instead of one. Furthermore, as it was sometimes difficult to synchronize the separate transactions exchange exposures might have to be incurred in any case.

Compared to the period from 1960 to the present day, the 1950s were a time of relative quiet. There were, of course, successive bear raids on sterling and French francs, but at least initially these were not of sufficient magnitude to overcome the defence mechanism of the central banks. Great Britain was able to hold the sterling exchange rate at its 1949 parity in spite of the Suez crisis and a bout of severe selling of sterling balances. France did devalue in 1957 and 1958, not entirely to stop speculation: the competitiveness of French goods in the export markets and a desire to protect the home market really motivated the decision to adjust the parity. Apart from the devaluations of minor currencies the 1950s was a decade of exchange rate equilibrium. Fairly low interest rates prevailed in most countries, so they had little effect on the external values of currencies. Any country which felt threatened by speculation against its currency had simply to increase domestic interest rates by a few per cent and the outflow of money stopped. It must not be forgotten in the present climate of high interest rates that in absolute terms an increase from 5 to 7 per cent is usually more effective than one from 10 per cent to 14 per cent when all interest rates are on a high plateau, in spite of the fact that the arithmetic ratio is the same. The effectiveness of this interest rate weapon was largely due to the low inflation levels in most countries combined with the only moderate growth of the world's economies.

Some rather simplistic conclusions can be drawn from French

and British experiences in this period. Whenever the French franc is threatened, France will devalue in due course but retain the initiative of the timing, whereas Great Britain tends to defend until the bitter end. This intransigent British attitude only changed in the middle 1970s. It is not our intention to comment on national characteristics, but they are often clearly reflected in the foreign exchange and monetary field.

The *fata morgana* of a dollar shortage materialized as a dollar glut. At first of moderate proportions, towards the end of the 1950s the outflow of US reserves became more and more apparent. For German politicians, conscious of the havoc created after the First World War by hyperinflation, the continuing inflow of foreign currencies into the German reserves and the effect these inflows had on the money supply was a worrying trend, so that it was not altogether unexpected when in 1961 the Germans revalued the mark by 5 per cent, and the Dutch followed suit with a similar increase in the value of the guilder; the close trade and financial relations between Germany and Holland strongly influenced the Dutch action. German industry, in particular the export-oriented section, was violently opposed to the revaluation, it was felt that it would cause German products to become overpriced in the world's markets and that imports would rise, thus putting the 'economic miracle' at risk. How wrong they were: the saying 'Success breeds success' held true in the German case.

The revaluation of the Deutsche Mark and the guilder opened new possibilities in the management of exchange rate parities. Revaluations were not new to the monetary scene; after all, Britain had for all practical purposes revalued sterling when the Gold Bullion Standard was introduced in 1925. However, to revalue a currency deliberately to stop inflation taking hold, and to make domestic output less competitive was definitely something of an innovation. The Bretton Woods agreement had been aimed at preventing the practice of competitive devaluations; such things as revaluations had not been thought of.

In 1958 the foreign exchange markets in Europe were freed from their shackles. Standard foreign exchange practices such as cross-rate dealing were once again allowed in most countries of the West. Prior to 1958 most countries in Europe had operated two- or multi-tiered exchange rate systems. The official market—the actual exchange rate—was used for trade and service settlements, while the free rate was allowed to fluctuate, though with some official assistance at times, to accommodate purely financial or investment transactions. For a time the United Kingdom enjoyed a multi-tiered system: blocked sterling, soft and hard dollars, transferable sterling and official sterling. In 1958, however, the strong-currency countries in Europe relaxed the rules and instituted one exchange rate, and this exchange rate reflected the IMF gold parity. Belgium has retained the two-tier system until the present day; Britain merged the soft and hard dollars into one investment dollar pool. By lifting dealing restrictions and allowing cross-rate transactions, the opportunities for technical dealing increased considerably. In the United Kingdom the banks were allowed to buy or sell sterling only as long as they covered their positions, with the exception of a small balance, at the end of the dealing day, whilst in other countries only the limitations imposed by the banks on their dealing teams held in check any tendencies to 'overtrade'.

The accumulation of dollar balances abroad as a result of recurring balance of payment deficits led to the emergence of the Euro-dollar market. In the next decade the international liquidity created by the Euro-dollars—as they were called—developed into a fully-fledged international money market and provided the ammunition for speculative bear raids on weak currencies. How the Euro-dollar market originated and obtained its title is now a matter of conjecture. The story goes that the dollar reserves of the USSR were placed with banks in Europe rather than in the United States through the intermediary of the Russian bank in Paris, the Banque Commerciale pour l'Europe du Nord, telegraphic address 'Euronord', hence Euro-dollar. This is as good an explanation as any. We must remember that those were the icy days of the Cold War, and Russia may well have preferred to see its dollar reserves placed outside the immediate American sphere of influence.

The *raison d'être* of the Euro-dollar market may have arisen from Russian need, but this does not explain its rapid growth since then. The real reason has become discernible only with the passing of time. Euro-dollars were relatively free of exchange controls as most countries protected the national exchange rate and money supply and were less concerned about extra-territorial activities in the international money markets. Furthermore the banks in the United States and other nations had to keep liquid reserves against their liabilities: there was no such requirement for Euro-dollars. Another reason was that United States banks could not pay interest on deposits placed for periods of less than thirty days, whilst in the Euro-dollar market interest could be earned on deposits with an immediate withdrawal option or for periods as short as one day. This offered the holder of dollars greater flexibility and earning power. Interest rates obtainable in the Euro-dollar market also tended to be higher than those for equivalent borrowing periods in the United States. All these factors stimulated a rapid expansion in volume, number of participants and transactions.

At the outset most monetary authorities, including the Federal Reserve Bank, considered the Euro-dollar market a temporary aberration. As soon as the US balance of payments returned to surplus the dollars would come back to the United States and the problem would be solved. Nobody even in his wildest dreams could have imagined that the Euro-dollar market would come to bedevil the international payments system. Other currency markets grew up side by side with the Euro-dollar market, although they never fully developed and their volume and number of participants were very much less than in the Euro-dollar market.

From revaluation to devaluation: 1961–1967

Despite the 1949 devaluation from $4.03 to $2.80, and the 1961 guilder and Deutsche Mark revaluations, sterling continued to hold the centre of the currency market stage. The withdrawal from Empire brought in its wake the loss of Britain's traditional markets; European and Far Eastern competitors invaded and the United Kingdom's share of international trade declined sharply. Excuses that Marshall Aid had helped other countries to re-equip, that war debts were hampering the economic recovery, that other countries were expanding their trade from a low base made very little impact on the hard-nosed currency operators. Explanations, promises and wishful thinking, if anything, tend only to make matters worse.

In 1964 a sterling devaluation was avoided, but only just. The

Bank of England's new forward intervention policy, together with some effective economic measures, turned the tide for a short spell: speculation usually fades away when confronted with a determined stand by a government or central bank. It will, however, reappear very quickly if this determination proves to be a sham. The 1964 crisis was to a very great extent the direct consequence of Labour's victory. Money men do not trust Labour governments, though whether their feelings are justified is another matter. Labour has an aura of prodigality, not unlike the Democratic Party in the United States, and had made too many promises in the heat of the election campaign. The currency operators went to work with sharp pencils and came up with the answer that sterling was 'a sell'.

When I refer to currency operators, I do not wish to leave an impression of a secret society constituted of anti-social individuals; it is merely an easy way of describing the whole spectrum of currency interests—companies with capital investments abroad; importers and exporters who wish to protect the price structure of their products; service companies in transportation or insurance; and many other business interests with a genuine commercial background to their foreign exchange activities. Currency operators are usually thought of as the professional exchange dealers in the banks; it is surprising how many practitioners there in fact are outside these narrow confines.

The support operations of the Bank of England both in the spot and forward markets held the line in 1964, but the support given in the forward market boded ill for the future. The great advantage of supporting a currency in the forward market normally lies in the fact that the reserves remain undiluted, at least for the time being. But in the case of sterling the professionals noted down the maturity structure of the Bank of England's forward book and when the 'roll-over' dates came along knew exactly how to adjust the forward prices in order not to be swamped by official activities. The market could have been criticised for taking advantage of a known situation, but any other posture could have caused the banks to suffer very large losses. Support activities became a fact of life for an extended period, with commensurate losses to the foreign currency reserves as it was not always feasible to roll-over maturing forward support transactions into other suitable forward dates.

Towards the end of 1967 the battle seemed lost, and notwith-standing repeated denials by the politicians sterling devalued, making the pound sterling worth only $2.40 instead of the $2.80 at which it had stood prior to devaluation. Why such a relatively insignificant downward change was made, after two decades of severe pressure on the exchange rate and consequently on the reserves, is difficult to explain. Possibly the UK government reasoned that in terms of trade this percentage was sufficient to bring about a drastic turn-round in her fortunes; there was also the consideration that devaluation would cause domestic prices to rise. But devaluation proved very costly to the reserves. It had been a foregone conclusion for too long, become a question of when rather than if.

In retrospect, looking at the events surrounding the devaluation, it is easy to find fault. There is no doubt that it should have happened sooner. Why did the Chancellor of the Exchquer speak in the House of Commons on the Thursday preceding the devalua-tion in ambiguous terms—it was an open invitation to last-minute speculators. Why was the 'bear squeeze' instituted after the devaluation instead of before—could the devaluation not have been postponed for a week, or even several weeks? Such a post-ponement, accompanied by a severe bear squeeze, would have cost the outright speculators very dear and might well have forced some of them to reverse their short sterling positions with a commensurate saving to the country's reserves. It might be appropriate to point out here that when a country defends its cur-rency, it takes or buys in its own currency which after a devalua-tion is naturally worth less. Thus to restore the reserves to an adequate level will cost more after a devaluation and any action which defends the reserves is worth taking.

The 1967 devaluation was not a repeat performance of the 1949 débâcle. Only two countries of some importance in the international context—Denmark and New Zealand—followed Britain's example. The other followers-on were of minor significance. Devaluation and drastic economic measures took sterling out of the limelight, it was time for a change of scene and the dollar assumed the lead part.

3. From 1967 to the present day

For currency markets to operate efficiently, for speculation to be possible, especially on a large scale, there must be opportunities and opportunists. In a world of separate national economies and currencies, with exchange activity taking place only to facilitate the movement of goods, foreign exchange rates would reflect merely the difference in the price of goods, assuming, of course, that there were few restrictions placed on imports and exports. However, in a world of intricate financial arrangements also covering investments, not only in plant or equipment but also in services such as shipping and insurance, exchange rates are affected by more than just the trade imbalance of two or more countries.

We mentioned in Chapter 2 the huge investments of American industry abroad creating and then stimulating the growth of the Euro-dollar market. All these factors, combined with the United States' balance of payments deficits and other money flows, provided the raw material for wheeling and dealing. The US investor who at some time in the past had bought with his dollars the necessary amount of sterling to make an investment in the United Kingdom might well become concerned about the value of his asset if a sterling devaluation was in the offing. What action should he take? Sell a sterling amount equivalent to his investment for a future date in the forward market at maturity of the contract, buy the sterling back to meet his commitment or roll-over the amount again? This type of activity presented the opportunity, but the opportunists arrived on the scene not by design or good timing but by sheer chance.

The banking explosion

Adequate volume and a reasonable number of active participants are essential if a market is to function properly. Until the early 1960s the foreign exchange markets had been the preserve of a few specialized banks in Europe and a handful in the United States. But with the expansion of American investment in Europe and the Far East, some of the US banks with no offices abroad became concerned that the competition would take over not only the foreign business of the US corporations but domestic relationships as well. To ensure that this did not happen an increasing number of large money-centre banks and some of the larger regionals joined the race and opened representative offices and branches, first in London and later on all over the world. With an eye on the Euro-dollar market, the American banks, as a matter of course, installed a Foreign Exchange department to deal in currencies and Euro-dollar deposits as a means of generating profits in the shortest possible time. It would have taken too long to get a positive income flow by making loans, for loans take a long time to negotiate. The middle 1960s was the ideal time for this kind of activity. The foreign exchange and the Euro-dollar cake did not require cutting into smaller and smaller slices; it grew all the time and it was only a question of deciding what size of slab each new arrival could comfortably digest. The miracle of the loaves and the fishes in a modern setting happened all over again. But this time it was no miracle, rather the beginning of the inflationary spiral which reached its zenith in the 1970s.

The central banks, and the Bank of England in particular, kept a wary eye on the new arrivals, since apart from the American banks other foreign institutions jumped on the bandwagon and established outposts in other money centres. And profit was not always foremost in their minds; quite often it was the ready access to Euro-deposits that attracted them. To the credit of some authorities including the Bank of England even the officials who were going to run the money market operations were vetted as to their suitability and experience.

1969–1971: the period of benign neglect

But for the watershed of the Vietnam War the dollar might have fared differently. However, as in most wars, the vast expenditure incurred by the United States in Vietnam and other Asian countries was financed by the printing presses in the form of budget deficits. How a war can be financed otherwise is not an easy question to answer: war and stable money rarely go together. With the dollar being the reserve currency *par excellence*, all interested parties observed and analysed every snippet of economic news coming out of the United States. There was a spirit abroad in the corridors of Washington which tended to ignore the message which came loud and clear from the currency markets.

The now gigantic Euro-dollar deposit market provided the ammunition. All an entrepreneurial operator had to do was to borrow Euro-dollars and with these funds to acquire one or more hard currencies. As long as the interest rates on the Euro-dollar borrowing were close to those prevailing for other currencies he could lose very little, as the exchange rates were still kept near their official parities. The entrepreneur would need a fairly good credit rating to qualify for a loan, but given this, it was a charter to print money. Fortunately there were few entrepreneurs operating in the markets, and the majority of the banks and international companies conducted their businesses in an orthodox and conservative manner. In fact, many organizations misjudged the situation completely and believed the utterances of the politicians, or should one say some of the politicians. Nevertheless, the combined strength of those who had investments to protect and the fully fledged speculators was sufficient to create the momentum which in 1969 caused a further German revaluation.

The year 1969 also saw a French devaluation, so it cannot be said that everything was going the wrong way for the dollar. The 1969 revaluation of the Deutsche Mark was particularly interesting as it was preceded by a month of a floating exchange rate; theoretically, though not in practice, the Mark was allowed during that month to find its equilibrium level in the exchange markets. This approach heralded the beginning of the end of the Bretton Woods parity system. In the process, the Deutsche Mark may have had a helping push from the Bundesbank to find its equilibrium within a relatively short period of time and consequently it was not a fair test of the floating rate system: the official intervention of the authorities made it a dirty float, not a clean one.

As a prelude to the German revaluation, a two-tier gold market had come into existence in 1968, one for official settlements between the central banks and the other a free market available to all commercial users with prices subject only to supply and demand.

The staunch proponents of floating rates—the free market apostles—do not favour the 'dirty float' approach as it interferes with the price mechanism of the free market. Their opponents will only submit to the indiscipline of floating at all if judicious interventions in the market-place ensure a degree of sanity. The question of who is right is academic, as no government could ever contemplate abandoning control over the external value of its money. Possibly a supra-national body is needed to accomplish this, in which case it might even be feasible to have one currency and thus abolish the need for exchange rates at all.

The half-way house of the German revaluation did not abate the feeling that more drastic adjustments were necessary if the international payments system was to survive. As many multi-national companies had lost money as a result of the revaluation, the number of participants in the currency markets grew daily. Few companies were willing to leave open liabilities in one of the currencies strong in relation to the US dollar. This involved the *hedging* of all fixed liabilities, aggravated by the lead and lag phenomenon created by genuine importers and exporters who covered any commitment in a strong currency and postponed conversion of strong currency-denominated receivables. Leads and lags present a short-term problem which cannot be extended indefinitely: eventually invoices have to be paid. But hedging, which may involve the conversion of assets and liabilities accumulated over a period of years and assimilated gradually in the monthly or yearly balances of payments, is far more damaging, since reserves are not meant to cover the accumulated investments of decades.

In spite of the revaluation, the pressure on the dollar continued to increase with practically all currencies appreciating against the dollar up to their intervention or support levels.

In May 1971 the Deutsche Mark and the guilder were floated, Switzerland revalued the Swiss franc and Austria revalued the schilling. A period of great uncertainty followed until in August 1971 President Nixon announced the end of dollar convertibility and allowed the dollar to float freely. The build-up to the grand finale, as is usual when a currency is devaluation-prone, was a crescendo of denials that devaluation was even being considered and earnest requests to the Europeans and the Japanese to revalue their currencies instead. We have said before that patriotism is emotional and that emotion is not a sound basis for monetary policy. The lessons of the past, however, are rarely remembered.

Feeling in some official circles still ran strongly against floating rates, even managed floating rates, and in December 1971 floating once again came to an end. At the Smithsonian Institute in Washington new parities for the major currencies were negotiated and some lip-service to experience paid. Currencies were now permitted to fluctuate $2\frac{1}{4}$ per cent either side of parity, and the role of gold was further curtailed. The official price for gold was also raised to US $38 per ounce. Furthermore, and in principle only, the conference agreed that official bodies would not buy or sell gold in the free market.

Now and then the points of reference in the financial world do have to be updated to reflect more accurately the current position. As the Bretton Woods parities are now so far removed from reality, today the Smithsonian parities are used as the basis to describe a currency's strength or weakness. Rate movements between two currencies can be distortive and for this reason countries such as the United Kingdom weight exchange rates against a number of other currencies in trade terms and supply an overall percentage figure. Reporting the position of a currency in this manner may reflect the overall situation more precisely, but is of little use to the exporter or importer who finds that within the official percentage change is hidden a much larger percentage movement of a currency in which he is particularly interested. As the Smithsonian parities are still a major point of reference we have reproduced a list of the most important ones in the accompanying table.

To calculate the sterling parity against another currency it is sufficient to know its dollar parity and to multiply this by the dollar/sterling parity:

$$\text{dollar/DM } 3.2225 \times 2.6057 = \text{DM } 8.3969 = \pounds 1$$

On the face of it sterling had by 1971 recovered from its bad experiences in the previous decade. Against the dollar, sterling

SMITHSONIAN PARITIES FIXED IN
DECEMBER 1971 (MIDDLE RATES)

Against US dollars		*Sterling equivalents*
23.3000	Austria	60.7128
44.8159	Belgium	116.7768
6.9800	Denmark	18.1878
4.1000	Finland	10.6834
5.1157	France	13.3300
581.5000	Italy	1515.2100
308.0000	Japan	802.5556
3.2447	Netherlands	8.4547
6.64539	Norway	17.3159
27.2500	Portugal	71.0053
64.4737	Spain	167.9991
4.8129	Sweden	12.5410
3.8400	Switzerland	10.0059
2.6057	United Kingdom	
	United States	2.6057
3.2225	West Germany	8.3969

had appreciated from \$2.40 after the 1967 devaluation to \$2.6057 in 1971, even though the picture looked less attractive when the performance of sterling against the Deutsche Mark was considered —DM 9.60 in 1967, DM 8.40 in 1971. Observers in the United Kingdom may well have been deluded by sterling's revival against the US dollar, the currency of the old ally and main trading partner.

1971 to the present day

Once again the period of floating was of short duration, too short to restore the balance of international money flows. The successful hedger or speculator does not change his mind overnight; it must be proved that no further benefits are to be gained. The world had also become painfully aware of what inflation could do to money values, and that domestic money values would eventually influence exchange rates, and in 1971 the inflation rate in the United States was on average much higher than in the strong currency countries in Europe. Currency operators had also developed greater expertise and a high degree of sophistication in market techniques. The application of the principle that early realization of losses and staying with profit situations was best had produced positive results.

Apologists for the floating rate system will argue that it takes time for trade and investment decisions to make an impact on the price mechanism of the market place. Opponents object strongly to such a simplistic argument and might go so far as to state that floating rates will tend in fact to move in the direction market psychology wishes them to move. Internal prices will adjust gradually to increased import prices, export prices will increase commensurately, inflation may then continue unabated and the currency become progressively weaker and weaker.

To list all the conferences and meeting places, names of individuals who for a short while commanded world attention and then disappeared, descriptions of new schemes, plans, systems—sliding pegs, crawling pegs, flexible rates, etc.—would fill a volume and contribute little to the discussion. Some of the ideas in another time and another place might have made sound sense; others were downright absurd. The Smithsonian realignment did not fulfil its promise, and after incurring further deficits in 1972 the United States was forced in February 1973 to devalue once more. The price of gold was increased by a further 10 per cent, but as this adjustment affected only official settlements, the decision to float the dollar was of greater importance.

In the long term it seems to matter little whether currencies devalue, revalue or adjust their external values through floating, dirty or clean. But, as Lord Keynes pointed out, in the long term we are all dead. A country which wishes instantaneously to reverse a fundamental trade or money flows imbalance will have to take the devaluation route. For devaluation to make an immediate positive impact the new exchange rate should be fixed well below the theoretical equilibrium level. The US example shows that tinkering with parities will not solve the problem and, if anything, will make matters worse. The management of the exchange rate in France is a perfect model of how the problem should be handled, not that the French approach is necessarily the right one from an international point of view, it has tended to be self-centred and ignore the consequences to others, but the French devaluations in 1957 and 1958 may have contributed substantially to the expansion of investment and general economic well-being in that country in the 1960s.

The monetary repercussions of the Yom Kippur War in 1973 were more dramatic than any other international event since 1945. Even the Suez crisis and the Vietnam War were only passing episodes compared to the oil embargo and subsequent multiple increase in the price of oil. For the first time, the Middle East oil producers used their economic strength to achieve political aims, and in this they were moderately successful. It took little imagination to convert the oil embargo into an opportunity to increase the price of the black gold when the taps were turned on again. The Arabs were not the only beneficiaries; all the members of OPEC (Organization of Petroleum Exporting Countries) gained correspondingly.

The energy problem had been anticipated a long time before the oil embargo and the price increases. Energy experts had predicted a world shortage for several years and the action of the producers only highlighted how close to crisis the situation was. The wasteful usage of a finite energy source had sooner or later to come to an end, and suitable substitutes found to avoid future catastrophe. As the United States relied to a lesser extent than other countries on imported oil, it would have been logical if the dollar had appreciated when the news of the multiple price increase broke. In fact, as happens so often in exchange markets, instead of strengthening, the dollar weakened. There was much head-shaking in Washington and for that matter all over the United States. Market reaction to a news item or a fact cannot always be explained in rational terms immediately afterwards; what appears to be an illogical outcome proves right in the end. But it is inadvisable to accept the superiority of market consensus without question and investigation: market action and opinion have been known to be wrong.

In this instance, the market interpreted the massive increase in the price of energy as a minus factor for the United States because it was felt that the United States would be unable to reduce oil consumption significantly, that at least in the immediate future there were no alternative sources of supply, and that to exploit

33

new energy sources would be a costly affair of lengthy duration. Given that inflation was running at a higher level than in the major European nations it was taken for granted that the US dollar would have to weaken in the currency markets, which of course it did. The United States' experts countered with reassuring arguments that oil in the very short term presented a problem, but that as the price was now right old uneconomic wells could be opened up again, Alaskan oil would come on stream any time, the exploitation of the Athabascan Tar Sands could now be considered, and other forms of energy—nuclear, solar, waves—would all help in the long term to solve the power shortage. Reassurance is never enough to satisfy market forces, and the dollar depreciated further.

The oil price increase presented governments and monetary authorities in the industrialized nations with a scapegoat for inflationary tendencies which had existed before the price was raised. In all the commotion it was forgotten that the OPEC countries had used the inflation excuse to justify their price escalation. Their argument ran that because of inflation in the West they had to pay more for their imports; to compensate for these extra costs they were forced to raise the price of oil. Apart from raising the oil price, many OPEC countries also nationalized exploration and exploitation companies and some even went so far as to take an interest in the distribution of their oil abroad. The increased energy price did not create inflation but it added significantly to the problem. Monetary upheavals since 1973 have been numerous but an overall solution has yet to be found. The European Snake established by the strong currency countries in 1973 is still operative although countries, for instance France, have joined and left the arrangement over the years. Britain joined for a short time but had to abandon the scheme very shortly afterwards.

Combinations of floating and loose snake agreements may in the long term provide the answer to the age-old question of whether or not to have fixed exchange rates. Until a country has its economy operating efficiently with a moderate level of inflation there is no point in joining a fixed or flexible exchange rate system; it is better to continue floating, or even to devalue.

The sharp downward adjustment to the US dollar in 1973 and **1974** helped to stabilize the dollar exchange rate against most currencies, and since then the dollar has appreciated overall, if only marginally. It is popular to look at the dollar relationship with the Deutsche Mark and reach the conclusion that the dollar is weak, but if we look at the dollar against sterling, French francs, Italian lire, Mexican pesos, etc., it is clear that it has gained a lot of ground.

In Chapter 2 we referred in passing to the SDRs, which were the logical outcome of Lord Keynes' 'paper gold' Bancor. SDRs, which were first issued in 1970, have for official settlements created another instrument which can overcome the disturbing effects of sharply fluctuating foreign exchange rates. As SDRs are valued in relation to a 'basket' of currencies an SDR holding will not lose or gain much in value. An attempt was even made in London a few years ago to start a deposit and foreign exchange market in SDRs, but the project never really took off, for the same reason that the Euro-bond markets in various units of account systems never supplanted the market for securities denominated in specific currencies. For a truly international currency to be acceptable to official and commercial interests a place is required where transfers and settlements can be made, and book entries passed in the international currency. A system which simply states that when a deposit is taken in one currency it can or may be repaid or reclaimed in another currency at maturity, without either the depositor or the depositary having to state what the currency will be at maturity, is definitely unsatisfactory. Of course, if the currency was known there would be little point in depositing an amount in terms of a range of other currencies. If a Common Market Bank could be instituted or if the IMF could set up a clearing centre accessible to the major banks it might be quite feasible to develop an SDR or other international currency market not essentially based on specific currencies.

In conclusion, if we look back over the last thirty years, we can see that Bretton Woods and the Smithsonian parities were valiant attempts to do away with the need for foreign exchange rates, to create a world in which one currency would be as good as any other. Unfortunately, it does not appear that the world is yet ready for balanced economies. With the expansion of the Euro-dollar market, differing inflation rates and the spirit of mercantilism still the mainstay of national financial policies, foreign exchange rates will be a part of life for a long time to come. Importers, exporters and investors had better come to grips with the subject: they will find that most of the time foreign exchange is not a problem and that it can be handled in a straightforward fashion requiring little expertise, since it is in essence but a question of two and two making four.

4. The organization and structure of foreign exchange markets

The organization of the foreign exchange market varies from centre to centre. In London, still the most important centre for currency transactions, the professional inter-bank market is conducted almost entirely over direct telephone lines connected to brokers' offices, the latter acting as intermediaries between the banks. The New York market, which is rapidly gaining in volume and expertise, operates very much along London lines. In London, as well as in New York, there are quasi-official agreements that prohibit direct dealings in foreign exchange between banks, unless the amounts are fairly small. Similar limitations are not usually placed on deposit activities in Euro-dollars and Euro-currencies, as it is felt that the banks should be free to place their money wherever they feel it is appropriate for reasons of reciprocity or security. For the brokers, the arrangement that all inter-bank foreign exchange transactions have to be passed via their intermediary guarantees a stable income.

In other centres, for instance Paris and Brussels, there exist meeting places, usually in the local Stock Exchange buildings, where foreign exchange business is transacted face to face at a particular time of the day. At these physical markets, on the basis of bargains struck sometimes with the helping hand of the central bank representative, fixed rates are set for a number of major currencies against the national currency. Not unnaturally this practice is called the *fixing*. The rates thus fixed are then used to execute customer orders previously placed with the banks. Although in a world of speedy communications physical foreign exchange markets are an anachronism, the fixing procedure for customer orders does ensure that commercial transactions will be effected at rates which cannot be influenced by any one bank. It would seem, however, that the large banks attending such meetings with the knowledge that they have large commercial orders backing up their decisions can effectively move the exchange rates in such a way that commercial transactions show larger profits on execution. In some centres, the banks also charge commission for transactions based on the fixing. As the fixings are widely published, there is the added advantage that two companies can agree to settle their foreign currency engagements using the fixing made on a specific day.

Exchange deals with banks and customers resident in the same country rarely represent the major part of the business conducted by the so-called 'market-makers'. Market-makers are inclined to be more active over the telephone, telex and by cable, quoting exchange rates to large overseas customers and correspondents. This international side of their dealings is very often also more profitable than national business.

In order to become a market-making bank, it is essential to have a 'good name' and a good name is usually associated with a large capital base and international standing. If the bank is not known internationally it will have to make its name known by putting deals in the market to attract return business. Smaller banks are not necessarily excluded from the market-making category, but in view of their size they may have to specialize in aspects which the larger banks deem unremunerative: minor or exotic currencies, broken or odd maturities in the forward market. Above all, a bank which is or wishes to become a prime operator must be competitive most of the time: it would be unwise to be competitive all the time as this could be construed as showing imprudence or a desire to overtrade.

Banks wishing to operate on a professional basis will have to take some risks. As bankers tend to be conservative individuals the terms used to describe these risk-taking activities tend to be euphemistic. A bank never speculates: its dealers 'take a position' and to take a position it is necessary to 'have a view'. Position and view-taking work as follows: a customer or bank contacts the market-maker and expresses an interest in buying Deutsche Marks against sterling. The bank can decline to quote because it has no long position or stock (inventory) in Deutsche Marks. But to decline every time a customer wished to buy Deutsche Marks would soon lead to the bank losing its status of market-maker; thus even if the bank has no Marks to sell, it will try to find out from a broker or another bank what the rate for Deutsche Marks is and quote a selling rate to the customer. If the customer finds the rate attractive he will buy from the bank a given amount of Deutsche Marks in exchange for a certain amount of sterling. The bank now has a short position in Deutsche Marks; it has sold Deutsche Marks which it does not possess. However, to buy the Deutsche Marks in before committing the rate to the customer might have meant that if the customer declined to deal, the bank would have remained long of Deutsche Marks for no reason at all. In this case, the bank decided to shorten in Deutsche Marks rather than incurring a long position which it felt was not justified. All the bank then has to do is to go into the market and buy the Deutsche Marks back, thus squaring its book. On the other hand, a bank which is constantly buying and selling foreign currencies, in this instance Deutsche Marks, might decide to wait until a seller of Deutsche Marks came along and balance its Deutsche Mark exposure that way. This action would, of course, entail taking a calculated risk, because if the Deutsche Mark strengthened against sterling before a seller turned up the bank would make a loss.

Sometimes short positions, as described above, or for that matter long positions incurred as a result of quoting to customers and other banks, are considered natural positions as they have not been taken deliberately, but are the outcome of normal trading. Natural positions can be views, but not necessarily so. If a bank deliberately goes long or short of a currency or quotes in such a manner that contacting customers or correspondents will operate only one way—either buy or sell—it is taking a view. 'Taking' or 'having' a view sounds more respectable than 'speculating' or 'gambling', and with experience and technical know-how the risk is considerably reduced. Dealers will also shorten the expressions 'long position', 'short position' and talk about 'being long' or 'being short', which can be confusing for non-traders as they could interpret it to mean that the dealer is talking about his height.

The individuals in the banks responsible for currency activities are called *foreign exchange dealers* or *traders*. The terminology used by each bank to denote the duties performed by its dealing personnel varies, although basically the organization will be along the following lines. In charge of all foreign exchange operations, and in many cases also of deposits in foreign and domestic currencies, is the *Foreign Exchange Manager*. In most banks the Foreign Exchange Manager will no longer work on the dealing desk but manage the department, ensuring an efficient organization and correct implementation of official and bank constraints. The man in immediate command of dealing is usually referred to as the *Chief Dealer*, although in some banks he may also be called the *Principal Dealer*. In the larger banks there may be several Chief or Principal Dealers, each specializing in a range of currencies or particular aspect of currency dealing. Under the Chief Dealer operate dealers who, in descending order, can be identified as Senior Dealers, Dealers, Junior Dealers and Trainee Dealers. These individuals will take care of the day-to-day business and refer to the Chief Dealer(s) only for matters which require policy decisions to be made or involve definite risks for the bank, such as taking a large position, executing a customer order before the cover has been taken in, cutting positions which have been taken for policy reasons, and so on. It is the dealers who will quote dealing prices to customers, give their opinion on market trends, and deal on behalf of the bank with or without the knowledge of the Chief Dealer, depending on their level of experience. Outsiders contacting a dealing room should always specify which section they wish to talk to, *e.g.* the Deutsche Mark dealer, the Swiss franc dealer, etc. It may well be that in some banks the Deutsche Mark dealer is also the Swiss franc dealer but, at least, it will not be necessary to be passed on from one dealer to the next before making contact with the right individual.

The banks are, of course, not the only market-makers. Multinational as well as international trading companies operate from time to time in the market on a large scale. By the sheer size of their orders some oil companies can influence the prevailing exchange rate; the fact that they contribute volume to the market does not make them market-makers; it is rather that they sometimes enter the market without having specific assets or liabilities to cover, which makes them important participants, particularly as these speculative transactions can be increased, rolled-over, or reversed based solely on the views of the operators in the companies. What stops them from being full market-makers is that they do not quote buying and selling rates to most comers. Some of these companies can be market-stabilizers—given when a bank has quoted defensively in order not to have to deal with the company, the company will deal on the side which the bank dealers did not consider vulnerable and then the company will hastily undo the transaction with another bank. Bank dealers tend to look askance at this practice, especially when a misquote is obviously out of the market range, in other words the rate or rates bear no relation to the actual market rate. Occasionally it may be healthy for a dealer to be taken advantage of, particularly when he tries to 'read' his customer. The knowledge that a customer is always a buyer or seller may be advantageous as long as the dealer does not 'load' his price, thus generating extra profits at the expense of the customer. When a customer 'catches a dealer out' it will undoubtedly ensure that another time he will quote a more realistic rate.

As the bulk of foreign exchange business is transacted verbally, the *meum pactum* ('my word is my bond') principle has to be observed or the market would be quite unable to operate efficiently. Human nature being what it is, large transactions in particular should be confirmed in writing or by telex immediately. This will ascertain for certain that the other party has accepted the order and that no mistakes have been made in the transmission of exchange rates, dealing dates and amounts. In the inter-bank market it is not unusual for banks to exchange wrong payment instructions and even to assume that they have dealt with another bank. To compensate the innocent party for loss of interest and inconvenience can be costly and any and every precaution should be taken to try to identify possible mistakes before they have been carried into effect.

The real end users of the foreign exchange markets are the companies which export and/or import raw materials, manufactured goods and services. Unfortunately, with the exception of the very large national or multi-national companies, they make little impact in the market in volume or effect. In comparison to the turnover of the inter-bank market and the activities of the multi-nationals, the number of transactions and amounts of the medium-sized and smaller companies are negligible. In many cases the fact that Head Office is established in the provinces may mean that the information service is not as readily available or as up to date as that in the main centres. There are, however, indications that the banks are becoming aware of the plight of companies in the provinces and are endeavouring to provide them with more market information and rates. This is a positive development, as the result of foreign exchange transactions can significantly affect a company's overall profitability.

Banks' attitudes to foreign exchange and currency exposures differ in many ways. Before the Herstatt episode in 1974 banks' foreign exchange policies ran through every attitude from irresponsibility to ultra-conservatism; banks who covered and matched every risk, currency for currency, amount for amount and date for date. 1974 was a bad year in the foreign exchange world. The bankruptcy of Bankhaus Herstatt of Cologne was the direct result of overtrading in foreign exchange, which would not have been a bad thing if it had turned out to be profitable. It seems that this bank took a wrong view and consequently a wrong position. In the hope that eventually the market would turn in its favour instead of calling it a day and bearing the loss before it got too large, the position was carried and possibly increased until the bubble burst.

In the foreign exchange market, 'after Herstatt' is another era. There were several similar cases in the 1970s, but they were not something new. In fact, the Herstatt experience may have saved the market from worse. Since the event, banks both voluntarily and through regulations forced on them have imposed greater restriction on their dealing teams. Even the most adventurous operators of old have had to curtail their gambling instincts. The huge amounts which were commonly dealt in a few years ago have now made way for more sensible ones. One would hope that the same situation could not happen again, but there will always be operators and banks who will abuse the confidence of their employers or the trust of their depositors and business relations. However, for the time being all banks try to give the impression that they are working within strict limits and will not **overtrade in spite of grave temptations.**

Apart from their functions of control and regulation of the

domestic credit supply, the central banks do also intervene in the exchange markets either to stabilize a volatile exchange rate or to stop the depreciation or appreciation of a national currency. In this way, the central banks are very much market-makers, as at times they will enter the market to buy from or sell to any comer the national currency against one or more others. In some countries the central bank has to provide a market in minor currencies to give importers and exporters the opportunities to cover their currency requirements. On the whole, central banks when they do try to hold the exchange rate find it easier to stop a strong currency from strengthening and more difficult to prevent a weak one from weakening further.

The media quite often confuse the foreign exchange brokers with the market-makers and tend to depict the brokers as currency operators, which of course they are but only in an intermediary capacity. Brokers act as simple intermediaries, their main function being to negotiate contracts between buyers and sellers at rates acceptable to both. In most centres the brokers are not even allowed to act as intermediaries for commercial interests, as the banks would interpret this as an invasion of their preserve and would react by dealing direct instead of using brokers. The brokers have without doubt contributed to the growth of the market by constantly badgering the banks with tempting though sometimes imaginary profit opportunities.

Dependent on the quality of the salesmen employed by the brokers, substantial business can be generated between banks. Whether intensive inter-bank dealings bring great benefit to the participating banks is questionable; nevertheless it helps to create a wide coverage of maturities and currencies which would otherwise not exist. As these risks are spread over many banks—in places like London a hundred or more—there is little possibility that any loss arising would be so large as to have a detrimental effect upon one bank. In the final analysis inter-bank activities make it possible for the commercial end user to find a market for un-orthodox currencies and maturities.

The role of the broker in the market-place is a subject of perennial debate among the banks. Many dealers feel that banks should be able to deal direct, whether for large or small amounts. This **approach might cost less as there would be no brokerage to pay,** and it might also assist the smaller banks which do not always get the best possible service from the broking fraternity. Some dealers, on the other hand, prefer the broking system as it makes their work easier. Instead of having to contact hundreds of banks they can leave this to the broker. Both sides can argue the merits of their case but it would seem that if we believe in free markets there should be nothing, not even a gentleman's agreement, to stop banks from dealing direct.

Market procedure also varies from centre to centre. In some it is the physical market which dominates, whilst in others the fixing tends to upset or change the pattern of supply and demand. In other places settlements of foreign exchange transactions take place sooner or later than is the normal practice in the European markets. Parties with a vital interest in a particular foreign exchange market should make it their business to familiarize themselves with local practices and conditions, either by reading the literature available or by contacting suitable banks for clarification. Commercial interests should never hesitate to approach a bank for information, in particular the bank they use for their normal domestic business.

5. Main factors influencing exchange rates

In Chapters 1–3 we devoted some time to the study of the origins and recent history of the exchange markets and exchange rates. Without exchange rates there can be no exchange market, although a market is not a prerequisite for exchange rates to exist.

A number of causes for exchange rate movements have been already enumerated, such as balance of payment deficits, inflation levels, money outflows, and so on. There was, however, no explanation as to why exchange rates are in fact necessary for international trade and investment. Exchange rates do not normally exist within the boundaries of a sovereign state. Prices for goods and services may vary substantially from state to state but throughout the United States all payments are effected in dollars, the national unit of account. Prices are simply higher or lower depending on the nearness of the market for the goods and the demand for them. It is obvious that housing will cost more in the New York area than in a small town in the Mid-West as land is in short supply; a few years ago there was even a particular brand of beer sold in the South-West which was so popular that it commanded a premium in other parts of the country. Similarly, some textile products will be marginally cheaper in Lancashire and Yorkshire than they are in the South of England, but all the same the price will still be expressed in pound sterling. Price variations within a country will be influenced by the fact that they are produced locally, shortages in housing and land, patterns of transportation and distribution, state and municipal taxation, and many other factors. But a dollar is a dollar and a pound remains a pound within the national territories of the United States and the

45

United Kingdom. Difficulties arise only when nations each have their own unit of account which is not legal tender or readily accepted as a means of payment in another country so that a value has to be set either by decree or through supply or demand in the market-place. This value or price is the exchange rate.

When foreign currencies are used to pay for imports from abroad the seller in the other country, the exporter, has to know exactly how much these currencies are worth in his own currency otherwise he will not be able to judge whether his trading activities are profitable. If we take the example of a US wine importer who has contracted to pay a French shipper US dollars, the exporter will have made an economically worthwhile deal only if the US dollar value of the wine after conversion into French francs still shows a profit. The dilemma would not be solved by the US importer agreeing to pay the shipper in French francs, because then the importer would have to acquire the French francs in the exchange market before being able to fix his import costs and to enable him to pay for the goods. So, in principle, unless there is someone willing to state what the French francs are worth in US dollars or vice versa, international trade would have to be conducted on a barter basis: I will take your wine and ship you in return tractors or whatever product is acceptable to you as a French exporter. Barter trade is cumbersome and not very efficient. Regrettably various forms of barter are becoming fashionable again because some countries do not have sufficient foreign exchange reserves to pay for their imports, but it is definitely not a satisfactory way of transacting international business.

Are exchange rates necessary?

The honest answer would have to be 'yes and no'. Yes, because it seems impossible to merge different monetary systems even on a geographical area basis. No, because some countries seem to get along fine without exchange rates. On the other hand there are some countries which find it hard to exist without them as they cannot use their own currency to settle their export or import transactions.

There are other nations, in the main the under-developed ones, which do not allow their currencies to be traded in the markets and where the parities, and the supply of foreign currency, are managed by the central bank or equivalent monetary body. These countries, of course, do have exchange rates but they are fixed internally only to permit importers and exporters to invoice in foreign currencies or make payments in them.

The fact that a currency has no external exchange rate does not mean that devaluation or revaluation is out of the question; if there are insufficient foreign currency reserves the internal exchange rate will have to be devalued or depreciated, and conversely will have to be revalued or appreciated if a glut of foreign currencies comes in. It is rare for countries with strong currencies not to have an external exchange rate; on the whole internal exchange rates make sense only if the intent is to protect a minor or exotic currency.

Whilst currency speculators can be blamed for changing or attempting to change the external value of a currency which is quoted in the free market, they cannot be held responsible when an outflow of the reserves occurs in a currency with only an internal exchange rate. If anything, the fact that a currency is not quoted in the free market and is completely managed by the central bank will make matters worse. As official bodies are not given to take decisions quickly even when they are of a vital nature, the outflow of foreign reserves may be worse than if the market-place had been in a position to show its feelings by adjusting the exchange rate in the appropriate direction.

In conclusion, it does not seem to matter whether a currency is allowed to float freely or is rigidly managed; when a fundamental disequilibrium shows up unpleasant measures have to be taken and the exchange rate brought in line with reality.

Currency areas

When the British Empire was in its heyday, the traditional pink colour on the map of the world which indicated these far-flung possessions also delineated one huge currency area—the Sterling Area—for a time also called the Scheduled Territories. As most of the nations in the Empire had currencies which were firmly linked to the pound and which in most instances kept their reserves in London, this was a perfect example of how currencies can operate together without any need for exchange rates. The exchange rates between sterling and those of the other nations in the Empire were fixed most of the time and any margin between buying and selling rates was there simply to allow the banks to cover their costs and to make a profit on any conversion transactions.

There are still today some countries which operate within a currency area and which either do not find it necessary to have exchange rates or have exchange rates which move only marginally over a long period of time. This type of inter-currency relationship usually requires close geographical propinquity and a free flow of trade and finance uninhibited by tariffs or other restrictions. In most of these inter-currency relationships one or more of the countries is a satellite of a dominant partner—Belgium and Luxemburg, the United Kingdom and Ireland, Switzerland and Liehtenstein, and to some extent the United States and Canada.

The origins of the inter-currency relationship between the United Kingdom and Ireland are of course historical and geographical. Ireland still supplies Britain with seasonal labour and the overall trade pattern is roughly in balance. To a great degree the flow of trade is also complementary. In Eire, United Kingdom legal tender is accepted as readily as the national issue. The same cannot be said about the acceptability of Irish notes in the United Kingdom but for a small handling charge most banks will convert Irish notes into English or Scottish pounds. A British traveller going to Ireland has no conversion problems at all.

The United States and Canada also have a special relationship, though it has never gone as far as a common exchange rate. Looking back over the last thirty years the exchange rate between the Canadian and the US dollar has in practice moved by a maximum of 7 per cent away from the 1 : 1 parity, which in exchange-rate terms is of little consequence. Canadian interest rates are frequently higher than commensurate yields obtainable in the United States; this results in a flow of funds from the United States to Canada, and since the exchange rate is expected to be reasonably stable for a period of time US investors may not even cover the forward exchange risk. This close relationship with its neighbour has allowed Canada the freedom to operate a floating exchange rate, although regular interventions by the Bank of Canada ensure that excessive movements are levelled out. As long as Canada can keep its economy running in tandem with conditions prevailing in the United States this currency inter-relationship will be of advantage to both countries; however, if one day a fundamental imbalance presented itself a definite realignment of the parity would be necessary.

There are some obvious advantages and disadvantages in such a close financial relationship. When the economy of the 'big brother' is booming, the smaller partner will reap its share of the benefits; conversely, it will be affected more severely when a recession or a slump sets in. The satellite country is no more and no less affected than any depressed area within the national boundaries of a sovereign state. Conditions in Ireland, for instance, will be approximately the same as in the North-western or North-eastern regions of England. As a sovereign state Ireland might even be in a stronger position than a depressed area within the United Kingdom, as it can direct investment, lower taxation, encourage public works, etc., which local regions in the United Kingdom would not be able to do without reference to the central government.

For the Common Market ideal to become viable, a one-currency area approach would be essential. The German might still have his Marks and the Frenchman his francs, but with a free flow of investments, labour and trade and as long as the issue of new Marks or francs occurred in proportion to the respective population numbers, the exchange rate between the two currencies would remain stable, and after a time both currencies would be considered *pari-passu* and used indiscriminately both sides of the border.

Exchange rates are needed to adjust imbalances in external financial relationships which cannot be corrected in any other way. The United States–Canada example is a case of imbalance in the respective interest rates. Why should Canada pay higher interest rates than in the United States? It is necessary only to cast a casual glance at the map and find that Canada, with far fewer inhabitants, covers a larger area than the United States. To develop its infrastructure and exploit its natural resources Canada has to rely on foreign funds, as it could not hope to finance all that is necessary from internally generated capital funds; thus to attract investments Canada has to pay attractive rates. From time to time, these rates will prove so attractive that large amounts flow into Canada, and as these inflows are either denominated in foreign currencies or the foreign investor has had to buy the Canadian dollars beforehand, the same result will be achieved: the Canadian dollar will appreciate, not because the economy is healthy but simply in response to market forces. The influence interest rates exert over exchange rates will be covered in greater detail in Chapter 8.

General and geographic influences

When we try to explain the relative strength or weakness of a country's currency, we have to look first at its geographical and economic make-up. Is it rich in raw materials and agricultural produce? Is it dependent on one staple crop or one natural resource? If it has raw materials, manufacturing capacity, a capable workforce willing to work and produce and ably managed, it must be reasonably stable and its currency will reflect all this and be stable and strong. Very few countries are in this fortunate situation, however; most have to import and export to exist at all, and as long as exports outpace imports in value everything will be fine.

The activities of the population of a country, either as individuals or as a group, can crucially affect the external value of the currency. Are the inhabitants demanding living standards which the country cannot afford? There are many ways to spend more than is nationally coming in: higher wages and salaries; ambitious social welfare schemes; a shorter working week; and longer holidays. None of these socially desirable demands are in themselves wrong, but as Mr Micawber said: 'Annual income twenty pounds, annual expenditure nineteen pounds nineteen and six, result happiness. Annual income twenty pounds, annual expenditure twenty pounds ought and six, result misery.' And as currency operators are Micawbers in their professional views any country which appears to be exceeding its income will quickly see that fact reflected in pressure against its exchange rate.

Less obvious factors will also affect the exchange rate. Managements might make wrong decisions, manufacturing products unsuitable for the export market, or producing goods of the wrong quality or design or delivering goods too late. When a country and its currency are under suspicion, the smallest news item or statistic that can be used to prove that the economy is not functioning well will immediately rebound on the exchange rate. Stable countries present an idyllic picture of social harmony, efficiency and quality of life even though the reality tends to be less ideal. This may be unfair, but that is what happens in the real world: there is no room for wishful thinking.

The Purchasing Power Parity Theory

In the 1920s Professor Gustav Cassell's *Purchasing Power Parity Theory* held great sway. It considered the effect of exchange rates on prices, and how prices would adjust to an unrealistic or unbalanced exchange rate, other things being equal, which, of course, they never are.

The theory operates as follows, and to illustrate the example we shall apply the fictional exchange rates set out in Appendix A. The reader should familiarize himself with the procedures outlined there before proceeding.

Example 1

If we assume that Country A is an example of economic and social rectitude and Country B is populated by a race of sluggards, it should logically follow that products in Country A must be cheaper than those in Country B. Both Country A and Country B produce motor cars of similar quality but it takes the workers on the assembly lines in Country B just a little longer to produce each car. Consequently, a finished car in Country A costs Ca 3000 and in Country B Cb 8000. As Ca 1 = Cb 2, a Country B car costs Ca 4000 and a Country A car only Cb 6000. If there were no restrictions prohibiting the import of Country A cars and transportation costs were negligible it would not take long for car dealers in Country B to tumble to the fact that it would be cheaper to import Country A cars than to supply Country B cars at a higher price, since in any case delivery of the latter would be slower as well. Under the Purchasing Power Parity Theory this particular phenomenon could not last for long, as the manufacturers in Country B would lower their prices and the import would then no longer be price-competitive; alternatively the demand for Country A cars would be reflected in higher prices and again imports would come to an end.

51

The theory is very attractive in its simplicity, though in practice it would seem more likely that the efficient workers in Country A would produce more cars and eventually the car industry in Country B would either go into liquidation or turn to producing another more acceptable product.

Financial and trade flows between two or more countries are usually of such a complex nature that the specific price relationship between various products will be difficult to define, as national habits and preferences, taxation and many other factors will affect internal price structure. Obviously, if the price difference between two or more countries eventually results in balance of payments problems, deficits in the trade balance and so on, the most likely outcome will be that in Example 1 Country B will have to devalue its currency or let it find its equilibrium level in the exchange markets. The Purchasing Power Parity level for Cbs would have to be Ca 1 = Cb 2.666, because then the cost of a Country A car would equal that of a Country B one, *i.e.* Cb 8000, and, everything being equal, Country A's export drive should come to an end.

Inflation, deflation, reflation, stagflation

The Purchasing Power Parity Theory, which cost some banks dearly before the Second World War, came to the fore again in the early 1970s, but in disguise. Up to a few years ago currency operators tended to look solely at reserves, balance of payments and trade balance but with the increasing effect of inflation on internal and external price structures, the purchasing power of a currency has come under the microscope once again. Of course, dealers do not look at products or even a range of products; they base their views on the wholesale price index and its progeny the retail price index—the latter in particular is considered all-important in judging whether a currency should be strong or weak. It is the overall percentage change that concerns the money men, whether the increase is at an acceptable level or is showing a steep, upward curve. A few per cent per annum increase in the cost of living can be associated with an expanding economy and in the 1970s levels of 5 or 6 per cent have been considered normal though worrying. Whether small or large, any increase in the cost of living is inflationary; it will usually result in demands for higher wages or other benefits as workers and managers attempt to protect their living standards, and this process may cause further rises in prices.

When price increases get out of hand terms such as 'rampant', 'runaway' and 'hyper' qualify the degree of inflation. The period of inflation in Germany during the early 1920s is always held up as an example of the havoc inflation can inflict on the man in the street, especially on those not in gainful employment; however, whilst the German experience of the 1920s was most unpleasant, not least in its political repercussions, the creeping type of inflation at a rate of several hundred per cent per annum which is not uncommon in Latin America may have longer-lasting consequences.

Inflation is rightly dreaded by both experts and the general public, but deflation can be just as bad and just as difficult to arrest. Deflation lowers prices to such an extent that production may stop altogether when it is no longer profitable and the resulting unemployment can be of such magnitude that it affects not only the economy but also the morale of the nation. The story of the 1920s and 1930s is in this respect not a happy one.

The effect of inflation on exchange rates is relative. If all countries suffer to the same degree, the exchange rates should not alter one iota, all things being equal. Prices in all or most countries would go up to the same extent and even the Purchasing Power Parity Theory would not come into effect. However, if one country exceeds the general level prevailing in other countries something will have to happen, and the something must be monetary or fiscal measures, or in the absence of these a down-valuation. The reverse would be true if one country enjoyed a much lower level of inflation than was the norm in others; its currency would very likely have to be revalued if the inflationary imbalance persisted for some time.

Using some generalization, it could be said that *deflation* is exactly the opposite condition to inflation: prices come down and if this a common feature in most countries and to the same extent there would be no justification for exchange rate adjustments. However, in a deflationary period it is tempting for nations to make their products more price-competitive in the export markets to take up the slack in the domestic economy and competitive devaluations will not then be an unusual feature of the international monetary scene. Deflation on a world-wide scale would require co-ordinated stimulation of the various national economies and this is the time when the printing presses might come into their own; deficit budgets would then make good sense, though 'stable money' advocates would deprecate this as it could spell inflation after a time lag. Naturally a country with a lower deflation rate than the others would equate with one having a higher level of inflation.

A country which has either voluntarily or by chance undergone a severe bout of deflation might decide to stimulate its economy by *reflating*. To counteract deflation there are a number of options open: lowering tax levels, encouraging investments, even raising wage levels with the hope that these stimuli will result in greater spending on home-produced goods. Too much reflation can solve deflation, but bring in its wake inflation, and careful assessment will have to be made of the overall effect of the financial encouragements given. The right amount of reflation should have a salutary effect on the economy, and this can be accompanied by an upward move in the exchange rate.

An expression which has gained acceptance over the last decade is *stagflation*. Stagflation is a very distressing combination of inflation and stagnation. Prices go up in spite of stagnant or decreasing economic activity and production, accompanied by higher unemployment. Stagflation is the term frequently used to describe the economic condition of the United Kingdom, particularly since the middle 1960s. The normal economic stimuli do not perform adequately in this kind of environment. The underlying causes of stagflation are rarely purely economic in nature, but more akin to a national psychosis, sometimes referred to as the 'lemming syndrome'. When this condition is diagnosed, the prescribed cure consisting of progressively stricter economic measures, has less and less effect on the economic and social behaviour of the populace. To eradicate the disease requires measures so unpopular that the incumbent government may well find itself out of office at the next general election if the system of government is a parliamentary democracy. When similar national economic conditions have occurred in Eastern Europe there has been some element of disquiet and the governments of these countries have sometimes had to bow to the will of public opinion.

What will happen to the exchange rate of a country suffering from stagflation is almost a foregone conclusion; in practically every country the exchange rate has had to be adjusted either by a severe devaluation or by engineering a sharp downward trend in a floating market. Imports have to be priced out of the domestic market and exports have to become so cheap that foreign buyers will compete for them. But whatever the eventual outcome, the side effect of a devaluation or severe depreciation will initially cause internal prices to rise especially for raw materials and essential imports. Will this be acceptable to the electorate? This is the dilemma the politicians have to grapple with and few have the stature to sell the concept to the population in general, let alone to the trade unions. For the government it is 'heads and tails I lose'.

Balance of payments

While inflation, deflation, reflation and stagflation are reflections of the domestic economy of a country and will be closely monitored by the money men, the first indicator of a currency's strength or weakness will nearly always show up in the balance of payments and as an immediate consequence in the level of the gold and foreign currency reserves.

The surpluses and deficits which show up in the monthly or other periodic figures will indicate whether money is flowing in or out of the country. The difference between the in- and out-flows will affect the reserves, nett inflows increasing and conversely nett outflows decreasing them.

In most countries the balance of payments is divided into sub-headings. Under the *Current Account* heading is shown the balance of imports and exports as well as the nett effect of services, insurance, transportation, etc. A further section will deal with official expenditure for military purposes, pensions, official remittances, and so on. The *Capital Account* itemises the effect of long- and short-term capital investments and official loans. A fourth section details the nett gold and reserve assets movements. This is the balancing factor of the balance of payments, but simultaneously it depicts what is happening to the reserves in the longer term.

Although investments made abroad could be considered as

assets and a plus element, as it can be assumed that either immediately or over a period of time they will produce dividends, in the balance of payments they are a negative item. If we applied the same principle to the balance sheet of a commercial company, a company which has borrowed up to the hilt would take precedence over a company which is rich in investments. Thus the make-up of the balance of payments could be questioned as being slightly unrealistic. The more owned or acquired the worse the position of country will be, as to acquire the foreign investments funds will have to flow out of the country. It does not matter whether overseas investments are paid for in a foreign currency or in the national one; the funds no longer belong to the country concerned.

When a balance of payments is analysed, distinction should be made between short- and long-term in- and outflows. It is obvious that short-term investment outflows can be ignored because they will affect the balance favourably in the near future. Short-term inflows are less reassuring, particularly if the balance of payments shows a deficit already and reversals could affect the figures detrimentally at an early date. Long-term investments should be considered in an altogether different light than short-term ones. Long-term inflows are definitely a plus factor, whereas outflows are without a doubt a minus element in the figures.

The outflow of investments from the United States during the 1950s and 1960s was one of the many reasons for the poor performance of the dollar in the 1970s. Investments made overseas are not a certain panacea: sometimes more money has to be invested than was originally anticipated and the profits may not be as generous or come as quickly as expected. It may even be found that domestic expertise does not travel well and that the overseas venture proves an utter failure. It is not so unusual for overseas investments to be written off.

The study of the balance of payments on its own would not be sufficient to evaluate the true state of an economy. However, over a period of time the way the figures are made up will give an indication of the future trend. A country which shows consistent deficits in spite of huge overseas borrowings is on the road to ruin, and a country which establishes a surplus only because of investment inflows, whilst showing a current account deficit, will eventually have to do something about the imbalance, and a reduction in the inflows may well cause a dramatic loss of reserves with a commensurate effect on the exchange rate.

There are countries—Switzerland in particular—which over the years because of banking secrecy laws, favourable tax treatment and political stability have enjoyed enormous inflows from abroad, to such an extent that measures have on several occasions had to be taken to cry halt by actually charging depositors instead of paying them interest. As long as Switzerland can continue to command the confidence of the overseas depositor and investor this is a viable situation, but if one day confidence should decline it might prove very difficult to defend the exchange rate—selling pressures would be enormous. The saving grace would be that the few commercial banks in Switzerland would be unable to absorb the selling impact, so the rate would adjust so quickly that the selling might stop at a new equilibrium level without much activity actually having taken place.

Consistent surpluses in the balance of payments for positive reasons, *i.e.* caused by trade and service receipts rather than monetary inflows, should strengthen the exchange rate against all currencies of countries with a less favourable or deficit balance of payments. Constant deficits will more often than not be followed by exchange rate depreciations, for only a slow-witted, dice-rolling currency operator would ignore the dire warnings of large deficits or surpluses and continue to buy the currencies of the deficit, and to sell those of the surplus, countries.

The trade balance

The trade balance—the visible balance—is if anything the most important component of the balance of payments. For some countries it may well be the most important part of their international receipts and payments. Countries like the United Kingdom and Germany, whose existence and economic viability depend on international trade, are judged more by their trade performance than by any other factor. Favourable or unfavourable flows will naturally influence the immediate level of the exchange rate, but without positive results in trade even inflows will not compensate for such a deficiency in the long run. The fact that invisibles are often expected to and frequently do not make up for the shortfall in visibles is not exactly a sign of strength for the United Kingdom.

The trade figures will also demonstrate whether there is purchasing power parity with other countries or not, subject to all other things being equal. Other factors apart from price distortions may, however, be responsible for bad trade figures: quality, delivery, after-sales service, etc. Sometimes the inhabitants of a country may prefer foreign goods because they are more desirable than domestic substitutes and because for some, particularly in volume, there may not even be substitutes. In addition, one set of bad figures should not be assumed to represent a future trend though it also should not be dismissed out of hand. As the trade balance changes minute by minute and an arbitrary date chosen to collate the figures may not be representative the results must always be corrected for seasonal factors.

A country with a healthy balance of payments and a positive visible balance is obviously in a better position than one that fails on both counts. Between these extremes there is a range of intermediate situations which can prove difficult to interpret and the market will often not respond to results which are not clearly understood. As I stated in my preface, my intention is not to look at the various influences on exchange rates in a purely theoretical light, but to look rather at the way market operators will translate them into action. Many times the markets will differ in their view from that of the economist, in spite of the latter's rational arguments. This is not an apology for the irrational behaviour symptomatic of all markets. It tends to prove that dealers look at economic indicators in their own light and that their interpretations may cause elaborate plans to fail miserably. Should we blame the policy-makers or the interpreters? Are the actions of the market self-fulfilling? Do the combined actions of the market operators perpetuate the conditions which official policies are trying to correct? Many questions can be raised, but few definitive answers are forthcoming.

Taxation

The balance of payments, trade balance, inflation and deflation, are the visible consequences of the fiscal and monetary policies adopted by a country. Naturally, other factors will make their contribution but we will consider those in Chapter 6. In the category of fiscal policies we can include unemployment and other welfare schemes which will eventually lead to higher output of the printing presses if the benefits are not geared to increased production. Fiscal policy—whether to increase taxes or decrease them, to tax indirectly or directly, to give import duties, rebates for exports and any other taxation measures which put money into people's pockets or remove spending power will be analysed, unless they are complicated, by currency operators. Only rarely will taxation changes immediately affect exchange rates, but there are times when the foreign exchange world will take notice.

A change in taxation which puts higher tax on the sale of goods and lowers direct taxes on earnings may be interpreted as an incentive for the workers to produce, for the entrepreneurs to use their skills, and in general for white- and blue-collar workers to work harder and hopefully save more. With the savings ending up in insurance companies, banks and other thrift-encouraging institutions eventually these funds may be used productively in new investments in plant and equipment leading to greater efficiency and higher production. Higher output should lower prices, create more exports, a better trade balance, etc. At least, that is the theory propounded by exponents of lower direct taxation. The fact that at the outset the cost of living may rise as the increased indirect taxation makes an impact is often ignored. The currency operators will look only at the effect on the inflation rate, and the exchange rate may suffer.

If the foreign exchange market can be criticised it would be in the same breath as the criticisms which would apply to all markets. The market atmosphere which according to its proponents should iron out supply and demand imbalance tends in fact most of the time to react sharply to events which are beyond the capability of individuals to interpret immediately and accurately when the news breaks. It could be said that market operators do not evaluate the general consequences of a certain event but rather how other operators will act or react, so that an assessment is made of the market reaction rather than of the event.

The market can be very fickle when it comes to analysing monetary and fiscal policies. If a country has gone through a period of deflation the market may cause the exchange rate to appreciate as soon as taxation, whether direct or indirect, is lowered. However, higher taxation imposed on the inhabitants of a country with high inflation will strengthen the exchange rate if it is felt that the taxation is harsh enough to discourage or halt consumer spending. Whether the exchange rate moves in the direction desired by the central bank or the monetary authorities is decided entirely by the market's conclusion about the adequacy of the measures taken.

Monetary policy

Monetary policy is less easy to interpret than fiscal decisions. But as it is fashionable for monetary authorities to show greater concern for the money supply than in the old interest rate weapon, it is necessary to judge the effect of changes in the money supply on the external value of a currency. A sharp increase in the money supply will usually send the value of a currency on the downward path, an increase in the money supply resulting from inflows may well appreciate the exchange rate. Just as an easier taxation policy in a country which has gone through a deflationary period may cause the currency to strengthen, so may an increase in the money supply.

Although few people would argue against the proposition that money and credit are basic to all decisions involving deflation and inflation, there is as yet no overall agreement concerning the definition of what is money. Most countries will include in M_1 coins and notes in circulation outside the banking sector plus demand deposits (on current account) held by the banks. Another definition currently in favour is M_3, and in general this is considered a more accurate definition. M_3 includes notes and coins in circulation outside the banking sector, demand deposits (on current account), savings accounts and, where they exist, certificates of deposit held by residents. Obviously M_3 is more stable than M_1, as the latter definition covers only a very limited range of money components. M_1 can show extreme volatility when depositors withdraw funds from their savings account and put them in their current account for easy access (whether they withdraw cash or place the savings in a demand deposit account makes little difference, as both are components of M_1).

One day perhaps there may be evolved a standard definition of the money supply which will make matters easier for the policy-makers. Economists may disagree in their opinions about the validity of the money supply theory, but currency operators have now been sold on the idea and when they notice a substantial increase in either M_1 or M_3 they will equate this with inflation, unless it follows a severe deflationary period. It would be unwise to base exchange rate decisions purely on one set of money supply figures; there has to be a definite trend before there can be any valid interpretation. Just like the balance of trade figures, one set of money supply figures can be affected unduly by temporary factors. The issue of large amounts of government stock could for instance remove money from circulation and give the mistaken impression that the money supply was under control. Though in broad detail all countries operate and report their money supply figures on the same basis, there can be serious deviations from the pattern which make it essential to study in each instance the way the figures are made up. In any event, no currency operator should deal in a currency without having good knowledge of the money market and banking practices operative within that country.

Though the money supply is all-important these days, the interest weapon is still in use. Monetary authorities like a range of weaponry in their arsenal and the interest rate device is brought out when it suits. Central banks cannot ignore the short-term effect money supply policies have on interest rates, and though they may try to adhere to a money supply approach, it is necessary from time to time to ease or tighten the availability of money to ensure that interest rates do not gyrate excessively. Monetarists are inclined to go for a fixed percentage growth in the money supply, and have less concern about the consequences on interest rates, but few of them would advise the adoption of a percentage growth which would have less than a moderating influence on inherent inflation. It would seem that in countries with severe inflationary or deflationary problems radical action will be required and that the money supply can be only one of the aspects to be considered and acted upon.

Interest rates

One of the theories which gains popularity from time to time, particularly during periods of large increases in the cost of living, is that interest rates should at least equal the rate of inflation.

There are several arguments in favour of this approach; unless savers for instance obtain an interest rate in excess of the level of inflation they will cease to save and might even be tempted to spend before goods go up in price. High interest rates, however, do tend to add to inflation.

Whatever the merits of interest rates matching inflation rates, it is obvious that high interest rates will cause a currency to strengthen, all other things being equal, and lower rates will affect the exchange rate detrimentally. If there is equilibrium in most of the economic indicators of two countries, a higher interest rate level in Country A will cause funds to flow to it from Country B. This should cause interest rates to fall in Country A until there is no longer any justification for transferring funds from Country B.

The effect on the exchange rate may also interrupt the flow of funds from Country A (low interest rate) to B (high interest rate).

Example 2

Assuming that interest rates in Country A stand at 0 per cent and in Country B at 1 per cent per annum and the parity between the currencies is Ca 1 = Cb 2, residents of Country A would buy Cbs and invest them in a deposit account in Country B at 1 per cent per annum, since in Country A their funds would not have earned any interest. If a number of individuals and investing institutions became aware of the interest-earning deposits in Country B, there would be increased activity not only in Country B to place deposits, but first of all in the exchange market to buy the Cbs. It would not take long for the dealers to become aware of the demand for Cbs, and gradually they would adjust the rate until the demand for Cbs stopped and that rate would be close to the equivalent of 1 per cent, *i.e.* Cbs would appreciate from 2 to 1.98 per Ca 1. At 1.98 depositors might be less inclined to buy Cbs in spite of the interest differential unless they felt sure not only that Cbs would strengthen further but definitely not weaken from 1.98, because if Cbs went back to Ca 1 = Cb 2 they would break even on Cbs bought at 1.98 invested at 1 per cent pa and at the maturity date in one year reconverted to Cas at 2.

This effect on the exchange rate might not materialize immediately and the original investor might not only carry interest on his deposit but might also make an exchange profit if the deposit had been placed for a short duration only. The 1 per cent interest rate and consequent change in the exchange rate in Example 2 were assumed to have been made over a period of one year to simplify the calculations. In Chapter 8 we shall discuss the effect interest rates have on the forward market and the complications of the forward mechanism and the interest parity theory.

A 1 per cent interest differential between countries is really insignificant. In recent years disparities of 5, 10 and more per cent have become the rule rather than the exception. It goes almost without saying that high interest rates are a visible sign of a troubled economy. Several of the economic indicators will no doubt show that a number of problems exist within the country. And if these fundamental imbalances are not solved very quickly, high interest rates will lead to even higher interest rates, though in isolation interest rates will rarely solve an underlying economic problem.

For the participants in the exchange markets, measures which increase interest levels substantially in one country can lead to disjointed dealings in the markets, as the dealers try to find a new equilibrium level. They know that higher interest rates will or should produce a stronger exchange rate, but it is not always easy to determine what exchange rate is appropriate. In Example 2, we assumed a one-year transaction with the exchange rate changing over a long period of time as well, but in the real market interest rates change constantly if not in one country then in another, and these frequent interest rate adjustments will bring about frequent exchange rate movements as well.

There is also the possibility that some currency operators, endowed with a fair share of scepticism, will feel that the higher interest rates are not enough, that they should have gone higher and consequently the currency should weaken further, whereas others may be quite content with the measures taken and be willing either to retain their holdings in the currency in question, or acquire assets if they do not possess any already. Without these contradictory attitudes and interpretations there would be no market, as it would be difficult to find buyers and sellers.

Any new entrant to the market should make a study of countries and currencies with very high or very low interest rates and compare their economic indicators, political stability, etc. He will find that the answers will be self-explanatory. What may seem high interest rates in most European countries could be considered very low ones in South America, where some countries have suffered inflation and interest rates of several hundred per cent per annum. Whereas 5 per cent may be a high level of interest in one country, 15 per cent in another may be low, so comparisons should be made, but no generalizations.

Indexation

Some countries have dealt with the inflation problem and relative interest rates by linking savings and social welfare schemes, and sometimes earnings, to the retail price index; hence the term *indexation*. Brazil and Belgium have used indexation widely as it was felt that this would lessen inflation over a period of time, though in practice it has led to the phenomenon of *creeping inflation*. Higher prices, followed by automatic earnings-related increases, result in prices increasing even further. As long as the increase in the retail price index is moderate the indexation approach may stop excessive wage demands, but when inflation gets out of hand indexation only aggravates the situation. The United Kingdom has not gone overboard for indexation and has only applied the principle to a few savings schemes; as interest rates are relatively high in any case this seems to make sense.

Foreign currency borrowing

Connected with interest rate and exchange rate levels are the problems which some international companies encountered when they borrowed strong currencies at low interest levels over the last decade. The fact that Deutsche Marks and Swiss francs could be obtained at rates several per cent lower than, for instance, dollars tempted the cost-conscious as well as the greedy and inexperienced. The interest differential was intended to compensate for any exchange rate loss which might be incurred at the maturity of the loan, and as some of the loans or bond issues had a life cycle of five to fifteen years, several per cent saved per annum would have amounted to a tidy sum, particularly when compounded. Unfortunately even the few per cent per annum when compounded proved to be insufficient when the dollar tumbled from its throne.

And, naturally, it had only made sense to borrow low-interest rate currencies—the hard ones—to convert into the high-interest currencies—the weak ones. The number of companies which fell for this sure-fire cost-saving approach included some of the largest as well as the smaller ones.

At first, when borrowers come in to obtain loans in the strong currencies, these currencies will either stabilize or weaken against the weaker ones, which may give the false impression to those that have committed themselves to these transactions that they have made the right decisions and it may even attract other borrowers impressed by the cleverness of the originators. Eventually when the borrowing comes to an end the strong currency will strengthen again, but once committed the borrowers keep hoping that the currency will weaken some time. In fact they may find that some borrowers either unwind their borrowings in order not to lose further, and others repay their loans, or hedge them, and all these activities merely strengthen the preferred currency even further.

Luckily, borrowers seem to have learned the lesson and fund their assets with the same currency even if interest rates are high, and with the changes which are taking place in accounting procedures this may provide the answer to the problem.

There is a saying in the foreign exchange market that 'one should never job backwards'. It is a pointless exercise, just regret for a past dealing mistake. However, by jobbing backwards and analysing why a decision was wrong, an insight in the market and one's own judgement will be gained. It cannot be stated enough times that past decisions, situations, conditions, history should be reappraised time and time again. This is the only way that similar mistakes may be avoided in the future.

6. Other factors influencing exchange rates

The study of economic and allied indicators is essential to interpret exchange rate movements, but serious students and practitioners should also possess a working knowledge of less obvious influences on the external values of a currency, for instance unemployment figures, and how they relate to economic activity and inflation, wage demands, and so on. We may agree with the monetarists that wage inflation is the direct consequence of excessive increases in the money supply, but it is also the old situation of the chicken or the egg—which came first?

Rumours substantiated and unsubstantiated

Markets which operate in a free and unrestrained atmosphere can be subject to pressures which seem to originate outside the direct market environment. In many cases the pressures are only anticipated and thus a matter of conjecture. In spite of abundant currently available supplies, commodity markets may increase prices because freakish weather has been experienced in the geographical area where a particular crop is grown. The weather has introduced an element of uncertainty about the following year's harvest: even substitute produce may then be priced higher, as it is felt that if there is a shortage in the most popular crop the substitute will also be more in demand. Sometimes these rumours are unsubstantiated, becoming common knowledge in the market before authoritative trade magazines and quality papers have even mentioned or explained the situation.

Such rumours are sometimes based on complete misunderstandings—Mr X propounds to Mr Y what would happen if there were to be a frost and Mr Y receives the message that there has been one. And as the story gets passed on from one individual to the next it changes from a mild into a severe frost and the cause of extensive damage to the crop. End result, a short-term price crisis until it has been established that the rumour is untrue.

In the foreign exchange market rumours tend to be discounted if they originate in a quarter which is known to speculate on future events, and has been found to be wrong on previous occasions. A dealer who states that a currency is bound to strengthen or weaken will be thought of to be 'talking his book', to have already taken a view in the currency and having therefore a vested interest in the event taking place.

There are occasions where unsupported rumours temporarily bring about the expected effect, but not for long if they are not backed up with concrete evidence; it is also not unusual for the market to react in the opposite direction to that which the rumour should have stimulated. It must never be forgotten that there is no smoke without fire, but before starting to pour water on the smoke or to take to your heels it is advisable to be quite sure that the fire has broken out.

News items in the media are inclined to affect market behaviour disproportionately, even when the journalist has made clear that his conclusions are not factual. The currency operators may doubt the veracity of the news item, or even disagree with the commentator's judgement, but the knowledge that other dealers will be reading the item and taking action will drive many into pre-emptive postures and what was subjective becomes fact. Headlines which leave questions in the minds of the readers cannot be shrugged off as so much moonshine. Over the years versions of 'Sterling devaluation?', 'What about the dollar?', have been responsible for major crises; as the central banks are practically duty bound to intervene in crisis situations to keep an orderly market, there will be money flows which when they show up in the balance of payments will confirm that the market was right. The market participants do not always appreciate that the figures have in fact been influenced by their very own actions.

Such serious repercussions from rumours and news items are really only possible if there is something amiss in the first place. It would be unusual for a strong currency to transform into a weak

67

currency overnight. There would be warning signals in the various economic indicators well before this happened. The market operators are too well aware of the psychological impact of information that comes to light and are forced to take evasive action. If no satisfactory confirmation comes forward it might be advisable to adhere to the original policy in regard to the currency under suspicion, given that no large exposures were incurred as a matter of routine.

Inexplicable exchange rate movements

There are times when rates appear to be at an equilibrium level with supply and demand seemingly in balance; underlying economic conditions may justify a change but nobody is taking the initiative. Then out of the blue a sharp adjustment takes place. After the event, market commentators will try to explain the inevitability of the currency realignment given the available data, past performance and future prospects, but whatever the belated excuses the impression can be given to a detached spectator that some 'funny business' has been going on. Dealings with insider knowledge may have taken place and political parties, usually in opposition, will hint at 'dirty tricks' and the immoral actions of the mythical speculators. It would be a brave man who would stand up and say that underhand dealings based on insider knowledge never take place, but the times when both prior knowledge and the opportunity to take advantage of that knowledge exist can be numbered on the fingers of one hand.

A sudden adjustment in the external value of a currency more often than not occurs in the direction that everyone had anticipated, if not sooner then later. So when the expected change does occur there are many willing participants waiting backstage to join in and add their ha'pence worth. There was a recent example of this phenomenon when in 1976 the Bank of England seemed to lose control of the exchange rate. Various explanations were proffered afterwards. It seemed that the Bank was notified of a large buying order for sterling and in order to ensure that sterling would not strengthen excessively it decided to enter the market as a seller of sterling. This was apparently misinterpreted by some operators as an indication that the Bank wished to drive the rate lower against the dollar, and the dealers, feeling that what was sauce for the goose was sauce for the gander, joined in. This may or may not be true. Whether there was a misunderstanding some-where does not make much difference now, but it temporarily put sterling under severe pressure and from being worth $2.03 in January 1976 the rate dropped to a low of $1.55 in October 1976; later on the rate recovered slightly and in September 1977 reached a stable level of 1.74 or thereabouts. Sterling recovered after the 1.55 episode because that rate was too low, or had been reached in too short a time, and there had to be reaction. The optimistic news later in the year about the North Sea oil flows helped considerably: any currency will improve when the forecast is that inflows will cure the balances of payments and trade at the same time, and even produce surpluses, particularly if these fortunate events are promised for the very near future.

Revaluation defence

Although a currency's propensity to revalue can be as strong as that to devalue, it is usually easier to postpone such a decision, as after all the currency is in a position of strength and a delay can be beneficial for the export sector as overseas buyers will advance their orders and payments to make sure that they do not get hit by the revaluation which seems imminent. Then the 'leading' of overseas buyers will add to the strength of the currency and make the revaluation that bit more certain. However, unless adequate measures can be taken to stop inflows from abroad, the revaluing country may find inflationary pressures building up which might be difficult to arrest later if left unchecked. As revaluations used to be such a rare event, very little has been written about them. Devaluation procedures and defence mechanisms make far more interesting and absorbing study material.

Regulations and technical interventions

When discussing the 'sudden adjustment' phenomenon, particular-ly in relation to floating rates, we mentioned that the 1976 sterling experience was not anticipated. In retrospect, it seems obvious that the stability of sterling at the time was a knife-edge affair, with Bank of England intervention in the market the sole reason for the balance which existed. All the ingredients were there to start a downward adjustment; someone had only to take the initiative. Whenever a central bank provides the balancing factor a build-up of speculative pressures in excess of the authorities' contribution will be sufficient to start the movement down the slippery slope. To stop unwanted currency flows would require combined and co-ordinated action from the major central banks, and while central bankers might be willing to teach the real speculators a lesson, getting the go-ahead from their political masters may be less straightforward.

Interventions in the exchange market by the authorities may not be the answer when a currency comes under continuous attack. A more effective way may be to introduce foreign exchange regulations if it is felt that an exchange rate adjustment is not justified. Regrettably, however, once foreign exchange regulations have been introduced it is rare for them to be removed altogether; quite often they remain, protecting a currency parity which is not viable and in need of urgent reappraisal. To create the least possible disturbance the duty to supervise the implementation of the regulations should be placed on the channels which are available to make payments abroad, and of course the banks are in the best position to be agents of such control and monitoring of in- and outflows. The more channels open, the more complicated the whole matter of enforcing the regulations becomes. The edicts of the monetary authorities should be worded in clear, straightforward language leaving the reader in no doubt as to their meaning. Regulations which demand a legal counsel to establish their true implication only complicate the issue. The Bank of England tends to be very experienced in this respect, possibly because in the UK foreign exchange restrictions have been a fact of life for so long. The authorities in the United States and in France on the other hand tend to use a 'legalese' which is not readily understood by the ordinary businessman.

Foreign exchange regulations should preferably be of the open rather than the hidden variety, such as the Exchange Equalization Tax imposed in the United States during the 1960s. This was a penalty imposed on US investments abroad and was lifted in the early 1970s. It did the job it was intended to do, effectively to stop investment outflows, but was introduced too late in the day and, of course, could not save the dollar which by then was over-valued. The tax was more acceptable in the United States than foreign exchange regulations in view of the market-orientated economy, and of course it meant a saving of manpower as it could be operated by the tax authorities instead of involving the creation of an entirely new government department.

Foreign exchange regulations, whether hidden or open, must be of such severity that the cost or danger of prosecution incurred by infringing them will be sufficient deterrent to allow the monetary authorities to stop supporting the currency. A combination of support and foreign exchange regulations can only mean that other and more lasting measures will have to be taken in due course. Regulations controlling money flows are necessary in war conditions, but in any case the market may then not be in a position to operate in the absence of buyers, or sellers, or both.

Indirect intervention

Although central banks encourage normal market activities in the foreign exchanges, they should always ensure that speculators do not by their activities distort a market which is really intended to accommodate the requirements of genuine importers and exporters. One obvious way of supporting the currency is to sell foreign currencies at a fixed rate to any comer. This approach can, however, have a disproportionate impact on the reserves, and a more acceptable way which penalizes the speculator and rewards the holders of the currency is to implement a *bear squeeze*. By raising the interest rates for the national currency freely available to market operators, those who are short of the currency will have to pay a penalty where those who are long will gain higher yields on their holdings. Naturally this procedure can be effective only if domestic funds are not accessible to the foreign exchange market, and to enforce a bear squeeze foreign exchange regulations will have to be in operation to arrest the flow of funds abroad unless there is a genuine commercial reason.

This approach was adopted by the United Kingdom just after the 1967 devaluation, and has been employed on a number of occasions since. France has also been very successful in operating this ploy. The implementation of a bear squeeze will force the speculators in the forward market at progressively worsening forward margins; the alternative is to stay short of the currency in the spot and to roll-over the position in short-date maturities at prohibitive cost. The speculators will then have to be very certain of their views and may even have to buy the currency back. The day after the 1967 devaluation when the sterling market re-opened rates of up to 2000 per cent per annum had to be paid for 'overnight' Euro or exchange sterling, and for the next few days prices of several hundred per cent per annum prevailed. If this bear squeeze had been put into effect before the devaluation very few speculators would have been brave enough to stay short of sterling for longer than a few days.

The genuine user of the market may unfortunately be penalized as well as the speculator, possibly more so since the speculator is usually better versed in foreign exchange techniques. All the more reason for the genuine commercial user to acquire an adequate working knowledge of foreign exchange: as in law, a plea of ignorance is no excuse for losses incurred through greed or ineptitude.

In the case of a revaluation-prone currency, the authorities can regulate the money market and protect it from inflows by imposing restrictions which in effect bring about negative interest rates. Holders of Deutsche Marks and Swiss francs have at times had to dispose of their holdings for short periods and have actually had to pay the recipient to take the funds. This was cheaper than leaving the funds on current account in Germany or Switzerland, and in any case they might have found no one in Germany or Switzerland willing to accept the funds even if they had paid them.

Such 'bear' and 'bull' squeezes can give the authorities a breathing space and allow them to effect exchange rate adjustments in their own time without speculators breathing down their necks.

One-way market

The one-way market, that is one with all sellers and no buyers or vice versa, frequently comes into effect when a currency is not dealt in volume or by sufficient numbers of market-makers and end users. This will most often occur when a minor currency is under pressure. If only a few major commercial banks exist in the country, when they indicate a lack of interest the sellers in a devaluation situation will find it impossible to dispose of the currency. Conversely, in a revaluation situation there will be no sellers.

Excessive dealing in such a currency may even make it unnecessary for the central bank of the country to intervene: the market mechanism will do the trick. The rate may drop or appreciate dramatically but no major out- or inflows take place and accordingly the reserves do not have to be utilized. Confronted with this situation, speculation will fade away and this may be all that is required to stabilize the exchange rate. Genuine buyers or sellers will after a short time come to the market to cover their needs and further help to establish equilibrium.

Leads and lags

By now, it must have become clear that though economic factors affect exchange rate levels, the supply or demand generated by realized or anticipated changes in rate structure will in turn influence the economic indicators even further. The interaction of economic factors with supply and demand create a ratchet effect, and the ratchet will let the wheel move in one direction only.

Leads and lags tend to provide the movement of the wheel. Assuming that the economic performance of a country leaves much to be desired, and the expectation is that the exchange rate will have to be adjusted downwards this will affect decisions made by importers and exporters inside and outside the country.

The country's importers will cover their foreign currency invoices for spot in the forward markets, whereas before they might have waited until the last possible repayment day to acquire their foreign currencies. Furthermore, to ensure that their future imports will not cost more as a result of a less favourable exchange rate they will anticipate their future requirements and import more than they need for current purposes. Exporters, on the other hand, will postpone the conversion of foreign currency receipts, as the anticipated devaluation may give them a better return on their foreign currencies.

A combination of leads and lags will very soon produce a deteriorating balance of payments and worsening trade balance. Imports will increase dramatically and exports slow down. Thus leads and lags that were set in motion possibly by only minor deficiencies will create a major currency crisis.

Trading partners in other countries, who initially may not have been aware of the situation, will read the press reports and take evasive action as well, which will increase pressure on the exchange rate and the official figures. Foreign importers who previously might have settled their bills promptly will defer payment and might even postpone imports in the knowledge that if a devaluation or depreciation did happen between the time of paying for the imports and onselling them to their buyers they might have to lower prices as fresh imports might be entering the country at post-devaluation prices. Overseas exporters may decide to invoice either in their own currency or in other strong currencies instead of the suspect one as was their previous practice.

The overall effect on the currency will be that it will rarely be bought but instead tend to be offered only for sale. Thus the market will be presented with professional and commercial selling of the currency and very little buying. The foreign exchange reserves of the suspect currency will be put in jeopardy and monthly deficits of growing magnitude become a fact of life.

Imports will command higher prices with a depreciating currency though there will be no compensatory movements in exports as these will be postponed by overseas buyers. Higher prices will cause deterioration of external figures in the balance of payments and also the trade balance, and some internal indicators, such as the inflation rate, will worsen.

All these unfavourable results negate the Purchasing Power Parity Theory; they should not really happen if the theory held good. And naturally under a floating rates system the immediate effect on the exchange rate will be greater than under a fixed parity system.

This type of scenario calls for drastic measures, and import controls may provide the answer. However, there is always the danger that retaliatory actions might then be taken in other countries and this may inhibit official decision. The leads and lags phenomenon has to some extent affected the United Kingdom's performance for a number of years.

In so far as they postpone their foreign exchange transactions, importers and exporters in the suspect country become speculators—with justification, however. In a depreciation situation it would be definitely wrong to pay for imports denominated in the weak currency as this would make the products uncompetitive should a devaluation happen sooner than expected. By leading and lagging, the resident business community could be accused of lacking in patriotism; however, if there are no import restrictions and if they are prudent businessmen they have no option other than to anticipate trouble.

Hedging

While companies which utilize the leads and lags approach cannot really be accused of outright speculation, it is a different matter when corporations make it a practice to hedge their foreign assets and liabilities whenever a crisis threatens. We should define *hedging* as the act of converting the foreign currency equivalent of foreign-denominated assets and liabilities into a more suitable currency. And these assets and liabilities cannot then be realized in a hurry. Let us look at an example of an American company which has bought a manufacturing outfit in Italy. The firm's capital, receivables and liabilities are all in lire, so it is exposed in lire for the amount of the US dollars originally expended to buy the Italian company. Of course fixed assets, like buildings, can be ignored as these can be revalued for the consolidated balance sheet at the historical rate, or the rate of exchange at which the US dollars were converted into lire to acquire the Italian organization. When there is growing concern about the future value of the lira, the US owners will sell Italian lire equivalent to their nett exposure in Italy, for some suitable forward date. If the devaluation or depreciation of the lire takes place close to the maturity of the forward contract the Italian lire can then be bought back at the devalued rate. Any exchange loss made on the Italian investment will be compensated by the profit on the foreign exchange transaction. If the anticipated devaluation does not take place, however, the company will make a loss on the exchange deal.

When a currency is under pressure, and it does not matter whether it is devaluation- or revaluation-prone, hedging will produce a volume larger than that produced by leads and lags. Leads and lags have, or can have, great detrimental effect, but hedging can create a worse situation. By leading and lagging companies can accelerate or postpone their currency decision for some time, but not indefinitely. Hedging may be a continuing situation, as some companies hedge every foreign asset or liability whether in hard or soft currencies. The cost of such hedging can be substantial, particularly if it is a routine operation.

Not unnaturally, leading, lagging and hedging will have a greater impact on weaker than on stronger currencies. It will also be more usual for companies to hedge exposures in weak currencies than in hard ones, as hedges entered into to protect an asset will be necessary only when it is in a weak currency, as it would be nonsensical to protect a strong-currency asset in this way.

In countries with rigid foreign exchange regulations hedging of non-trade-related liabilities in the stronger currencies will normally not be allowed. This should be sufficient reason for investors not to acquire commitments in the strong currencies.

The terms 'hedging' and 'covering' are often confused. *Covering* is a simple foreign exchange transaction which converts receivables and items due for payment in a foreign currency in the forward markets. Covering ensures that the value of a trade or service transaction is definitely fixed. Hedging, as explained above, is implemented to protect the value of an asset or liability which cannot or may never be realized.

If an importer resident in the United Kingdom buys a machine tool from a Swiss manufacturer and payment for the import is due in Swiss francs in three months' time, by contracting for the purchase of Swiss francs against sterling with a UK bank the importer will have covered his Swiss franc commitment, the price of the machine tool is now fixed in sterling terms. The importer has acted in a conservative manner by covering the exchange risk. If he had left the risk outstanding he would have speculated either on the Swiss franc weakening against sterling, or that the cost of the forward cover would amount to more than the probable movement in the Swiss franc/sterling exchange rate over the period. If all importers in the United Kingdom adopted the 'wait and see' attitude to foreign exchange exposures, any untoward rumour or indication of a possible devaluation or depreciation of sterling might result in all importers buying their foreign currencies at the same time with an immediate detrimental effect on sterling's external value.

Companies can cover their trading exposures at the earliest possible moment, or take the attitude that over a period of time, by always executing foreign exchange transactions at the latest available date, what is lost on the swings will be gained back on the roundabouts. However, as these swings and roundabouts may not operate in the same financial year, wild fluctuations in company profitability could result.

The practice of hedging has been condemned by some experts as being outright speculation against the host country. An international company acquires an asset in a country: as long as everything is in their favour they will not hedge but the moment there is a possibility that the value of the asset may be threatened by a currency depreciation they will establish a hedge which will have a detrimental impact. If sufficient overseas investors operate in this manner the outcome is fairly certain. Some pre-war writers consider this aspect of hedging as an immoral activity; unfortunately, morals and business interests do not always coincide, and in any event the company's stockholders might not approve of business decisions which are morally right but negatively influence profits.

The hedging of investments in securities is difficult to explain or to excuse; the right decision would probably be to disinvest, as the hedge may have to be carried forward indefinitely and the income flow on the investment may be unfavourably affected by the currency depreciation of the host country. On the other hand, an active investment in an operating company engaged in export transactions from the host country could show increased profits, as the devaluation of the host currency might make export prices more competitive. Devaluations may set in motion a fall of share prices on the domestic Stock Exchange, particularly for fixed-interest investments. If in spite of everything a hedge was established, it would have to be for an amount in excess of the investment, thus allowing for yield deficiencies and loss on selling of the securities. However, even this might not be sufficient, and the best solution would have been to sell the securities before the currency adjustment occurred. Similarly, to hedge an investment in an operating company which manufactures only for the domestic market will not necessarily protect future profit flow, which may well be less when restrictive measures such as price controls freeze earnings.

Whether to hedge or not is closely linked to accounting practices in the country of the parent company. We shall devote some time to this aspect in Chapter 11.

Very short-term hedges may be necessary to protect the immediate value of an overseas investment, but to protect a long-term asset all the time can be costly and should be considered only if not to do so might adversely affect the parent company's balance sheet and create grounds for misinterpretation by investment analysts. It will also be necessary to compare the cost of the hedge with the current or anticipated profit flows. If it is anticipated that the hedge cost is nearly as large as the profits generated in the country it might be better if this is possible to dispose of the investment and have the company represented via agents or whatever alternative is considered suitable. Companies operating world-wide can take the view that such losses are usually counter-balanced by profits in other countries and that overall it is better to absorb temporary losses immediately than to have executives' time wasted in protecting long-term currency resources. Small companies operating in a limited number of countries are more vulnerable than the multi-national organizations given that the latter are established in a representative range of countries. For there to be strong currencies there must also be weak ones.

We shall refer to exposure management in multi-national companies in Chapter 11, but it may be worth while to point out here that some European companies when they make investments abroad in operating companies do not incorporate these investments into the parent company balance sheet and look only to a positive cashflow from the overseas investment. This may not appeal to companies which need the overseas investment incorporated in the parent balance sheet to improve its figures, but it seems quite a conservative approach for companies with ample cash reserves and other resources. In other words, they write off the investment almost from Day 1.

Foreign exchange studies in the United States tend to concentrate on the practice of hedging and accounting and economic exposure management, whereas in Europe the accent is on covering. Furthermore the United States' approach tends—after some bitter experiences—to favour the no-risk/netting-out system, which to some extent overcomes the foreign exchange dilemma, but at the same time also removes comparisons of pricing and profit opportunities.

Hedging can have a far greater effect on the exchange rate than leads and lags, or for that matter any other speculative activity whether justified or not. As hedging involves the temporary selling or buying of currency equivalents of assets and liabilities accumulated over a period of years if not decades, no official reserves are available to supply or absorb these flows in a very short time. Thus countries with many investments in other countries will be affected positively or negatively more than those engaged only in international trade. The events of the last decade and the volatility of the currency markets have shown the results of hedging activities to be more dramatic than those of purely speculative activity.

Reserve currencies and cross-rate influences

Reserve currencies in particular can be detrimentally affected by foreign exchange transactions which use these currencies as a means of buying or selling others. The exchange rates of reserve currencies will quite often then be affected, though the amounts eventually nett out.

This technical influence operates along the following lines. Assuming the operators are concerned about the future value of the pound they can decide to sell pounds for a number of reasons: hedging, leading and lagging, and outright speculation. As the main exchange market for sterling is expressed in dollar terms, the dealers will in the first instance sell sterling against US dollars. This may result in the dollar strengthening against sterling. As this may not be a welcome event to the British authorities, the Bank of England may enter the market to stabilize the exchange rate and thus the dollar against sterling will strengthen less than it would have done if the rate had reflected supply and demand. As the operators may wish to convert into the strongest currency available at the time (and let us say that this is the Deutsche Mark), the next step will be to sell dollars for Deutsche Marks and once this has been accomplished the currency operator(s) will have obtained the desired position. The dealers have sold sterling and bought Deutsche Marks; the dollar was acting only as an agent currency. However, in this situation it is unlikely that the German authorities presented with a demand for the Deutsche Mark will intervene in the market, as this would enable the speculators to buy Deutsche Marks at a preferential rate. Instead the rate will be allowed to adjust to the demand for the Deutsche Mark and thus the dollar will weaken against the Deutsche Mark.

Even though the underlying market interest, sterling against Deutsche Marks, should not have influenced the position of the dollar, the intervention of the Bank of England and the absence of support for the dollar in Germany or the US has caused the dollar to weaken. If this weakening is noticed and misinterpreted by other market participants, further pressures may develop against the dollar although there was no justification for this happening. The adjustment of the dollar/Deutsche Mark exchange rate was purely technical and did not indicate a weakening of the dollar. This is the type of indirect influence a reserve currency has to cope with and could have been avoided only by central bank co-operation. If the market mechanism could have operated by floating freely, both in dollars/sterling and Deutsche Marks/dollars, or if for that matter both exchange rates against the dollar were supported to the same extent, the dollar/Deutsche Mark rate would have remained at the equilibrium level with the dollar/sterling point.

Example 3

The technical adjustment in the exchange rate of the reserve currency may work its way through as follows. If sellers of Currency Ca are accommodated by the authorities at Ca 1 = Cb 2, or by coincidence there are natural sellers of Cbs against Cas in the market the rate for Cbs might remain at the equilibrium level of Cb 2. However, if then the buyers of Cbs turn round and convert them into Ccs either by buying Ccs in Country B at Cb 0.40 = Cc 1 or selling Cbs in Country C at Cc 2.50 = Cb 1 without the authorities in either country supporting the respective exchange rates, the rates may move Cb 0.41 = Cc 1, or to whatever level the rate due to demand met by a grudging supply will fall. A commensurate adjustment would of course also take place in Country C.

At the end of the cross-currency movements, Cas will have retained their original exchange value against Cbs, *i.e.* Ca 1 = Cb 2, although Ccs have appreciated to Cb 0.41 and Cbs depreciated to Cc 2.439, or whatever level was reached. Thus the reserve currency has absorbed the impact of the user currencies.

Had there been an active market in Ccs against Cas, Cbs might not have changed against Ccs, whereas Cas might have weakened against Ccs to let us say Ca 1 = Cc 4.87.

These cross-currency dealings are difficult to monitor and may give rise to news items which misinterpret the situation completely. The situation in Example 3 might have been reported as a definite strengthening of Ccs against Cbs with Cas remaining static. For this reason such news should be discounted. 'Selling pressure against the dollar from Sweden or Switzerland' may indirectly be caused by buying interests in one or more other currencies which have escaped the attention of the market. To some extent connected with such third-country movements is the question of the number of participants and market volume. If the market turns seller of a currency a rate may move very rapidly without much trading going on, but if then the market changes its attitude and adopts a buying position, even though the amounts originally sold equal the amounts bought, it does not follow that the exchange rate will return to the former level. It is quite possible that the exchange rate will strengthen less or strengthen more than the original level, as the market resists or accepts the movement. In other words, many more sellers may have transacted business than appear later to absorb the buying pressure or vice versa.

This technical feature of the exchange market, and for that matter of all markets, is not normally understood by the outsider. The layman tends to think that because a currency has weakened and then strengthens the fact that the same amount is transacted either way will produce the same result, *i.e.* the exchange rate will return to its previous level. In foreign exchange dealing and exchange rate fluctuations a balance in amounts and number of transactions will not necessarily find the currency equilibrium. The market operators can influence the outcome by either the sellers on the one side or the buyers on the other being more aggressive, thus distorting the rate structure.

7. Spot exchange rates

What is 'spot'?

When an interested party contacts a 'market-maker' and expresses the wish to buy or sell a foreign currency amount, and does not state the delivery date, the quoting bank will without hesitation show its buying and selling prices for 'spot' settlement. It would be unwise for participants, even for professionals, to operate in this slipshod fashion: obviously the date should be mentioned, unless the inquirer knows what 'spot' signifies when requesting the spot rates. Precision and accuracy are essential in foreign exchange dealings; short cuts will lead only to costly errors.

To ask for the spot rate is synonymous to asking for the exchange rate of a currency. The spot rate forms the basis for all transactions involving the purchase or sale of one currency against another. The spot rate is all-important, and quotations for delivery or settlement on dates other than the 'spot' date will be calculated in relation to the base or 'spot' rate. For example, to sell or buy a currency forward for delivery in six months' time, the spot rate will be adjusted by adding or subtracting the margin which is appropriate for this time span. Incidentally, some readers in North America may find it easier to substitute 'future' for 'forward', as the forward market is referred to as the 'futures market' in the United States though the term 'forward' is slowly gaining acceptance. The importance of forward exchange rates will be discussed in Chapter 8; suffice it to state here that some currency experts are of the opinion that the six months' rate for a currency may reflect its true worth more accurately than the spot rate. However, as the spot rate is the base rate for all transactions and more visible than the forward rates to the general public, it cannot be ignored altogether.

To deal for 'spot' does not mean immediate settlement. In the main money markets—London, New York, Frankfurt, Paris— it will indicate that delivery or settlement will be made in two clear, business, working or banking days' time. There are some centres, especially in the Far East, which deal for delivery the following day, and some for same-day or cash settlement. In these exceptional cases, whatever day is the normal settlement day is also the 'spot' date.

Given that delivery is made in a later time zone, cash or value same day and next day are quite feasible, but then the contacting party should make the preferred date known before a bargain is struck as the spot rate will have to be adjusted to reflect same-day or next-day settlement. As some banking systems in Europe require notice of payment or transfer on the previous business day value, same-day or cash transactions in European currencies apart from the pound sterling are rare, and where they are possible the price may well be less competitive than the spot rate.

The market in Europe, and its offspring in New York, originated in the days before regular air services and efficient telephone connections existed. Urgent messages had to be sent by wire through cable companies and this took time. Cables were a relatively expensive way of sending messages, and to cheapen the process they were encoded and normally sent overnight for delivery the following morning. The cable companies gave a preferential rate for the overnight service as it could be handled in the off-peak period. Some old foreign exchange terms originating during those days are still in use: one of them is 'cable', which still describes the exchange rate for US dollars against sterling. Inquirers may still ask 'What is your cable?', and be given the dollar/sterling spot rate.

With such slow communication in the early days of the market, it must have made sense to deal for delivery at a later date, thus allowing the contracting parties to process the paperwork, make sure that details and instructions agreed properly and at the same time giving them the opportunity to use the cheapest available means of transmitting their payment instructions. There was also an active market in *Mail Transfers*, 'MTs', which later became

Air Mail Transfers, but this area of the exchange market was used only for minor amounts.

The later date which seemed most appropriate was the spot date, particularly for settlements in the United States. Since then the spot date has become the settlement date for most exchange transactions even in Europe and the Far East.

Definition of 'spot date'

What is meant by 'two clear business, working or banking days'? Let us first look at the spot practice as it operates in the London market. Other centres which have adopted the same principle may differ from London as to the exact spot date because of intervening holidays, etc.

In the London market, a spot transaction, concluded on the transaction date Monday, would have to be settled on the following Wednesday, as long as the Tuesday is not a holiday in England. Naturally, if the transaction involved the exchange of US dollars for sterling, and the Wednesday happened to fall on a New York holiday, if both London and New York are open for business, Thursday will be the spot or settlement day. As a foreign exchange transaction consists of the exchange of one currency for another, the centres where the currencies have to be handed over or paid will both have to be open for business, otherwise the essential *valeur compensée* (compensated value) principle could not operate. By compensated value is meant that two parties to a contract deliver the currencies at the same time; thus at least in theory there is no credit risk. In practice, of course, it is impossible to make payment in New York and London at the same time. The sterling settlement will have been made before the dollar one for the simple reason that New York opens for business about the time that the London banks close their doors. What 'compensated value' does achieve is that neither party to a transaction loses out on the use of their funds. The dollars and sterling can be utilized for other purposes on the same value date.

An exception to the compensated value rule would exist when a customer instead of taking delivery of, let us say, dollars in New York requests the dealing bank to issue a dollar cheque in his favour or that of another beneficiary. In this instance, it would not matter whether the New York market was open on the day of issuance as it is most unlikely that the cheque would be presented in New York that very day. And there is even less risk of this happening if the cheque is payable at the counters of the London bank. If the cheque is presented in London, the bank will either have to buy the dollar cheque against sterling, in which case there is no dollar payment at all, or payment will have to be made in New York to whatever party has been indicated by the beneficiary. The 'compensated value' principle is still operative, as the bank will have had to leave a long balance with its New York correspondent if the cheque is drawn on New York and thus loses effective use of the dollar balances left to meet the cheque.

What happens to the spot date when a weekend intervenes? As the banks are closed on Saturdays and Sundays in the United Kingdom, a foreign exchange transaction entered into on a Thursday or Friday will be for spot Monday or Tuesday respectively so long as there are no holidays in the United Kingdom on Friday or Monday and in the case of dollars New York is open for business on Monday and Tuesday. Intervening holidays in the foreign-settlement centre will not affect the issue; the two days are decided by the open days in the dealing centre.

In dealings involving parties in different countries, uncertainty as to the appropriate spot date can arise. The spot date in Frankfurt or New York is not necessarily the same as in London. To make sure that there is no misunderstanding about the spot date, any request for a spot quotation should be accompanied by the spot date as interpreted by the inquiring party, e.g. 'How do you quote spot (date) dollar/sterling?' or 'What is your spot (date) dollar/Deutsche Marks?' In the absence of this clarification, the onus is on the contracting party. If a German bank contacts a London correspondent and simply requests 'What is spot cable or dollar/sterling?' and it so happens that the spot date in Germany differs from the London one the German bank will be committed to execute the transaction if it agrees to deal after obtaining the British quotation and only afterwards finds out that the British bank has dealt for a different spot date. The initiator of a transaction who is careless in the wording of his request is the offending party when a misunderstanding arises. In most cases when this kind of mistake occurs, both parties will reach an amicable settlement, but it is the offending party that bears any extra cost. If the error comes to light after the contracting parties have executed their payments, the settlement of interest on overdrafts incurred, in this instance by the London bank, would have to be borne by the German bank. Even if the initiating bank or customer does not specify the spot date, the bank executing the transaction should before the communication is concluded repeat all the details including the date: this may be sufficient to avoid a mistake causing inconvenience to one of the parties.

In the final analysis, the spot rate is also a forward rate, and some central banks will allow spot positions to be excluded from balances and overdrafts carried abroad as it is felt that by the time the spot date comes along the bank may have amended its open positions to within the allowable limits set by the authorities. Most banks that deal actively in spot will adjust the position when it becomes value next day (or value tomorrow) and in the case of sterling and US dollars even value same day. Excessive balances or shortfalls will be adjusted by executing an overnight or tomorrow next day swap, and how these are arrived at will be explained in Chapter 8 on forward rates.

Quotations in other currency terms

When a German bank contacts a New York bank, which exchange rate will be appropriate—the New York quotation in US dollars or the German quotation in Deutsche Marks? Again it is a question of who takes the initiative. If a German bank contacts a bank in New York and does not stipulate in which currency it would like the quotation to be made, it is quite possible that the US bank will quote in US dollar terms. If the German bank preferred to obtain a quote in Deutsche Mark terms, the New York bank might oblige but might widen the margin between its buying and selling price for Deutsche Marks.

Furthermore, as the German bank wishes to sell or buy US dollars whilst the US bank would be mainly interested in buying and selling Deutsche Marks, the bank in New York would of course prefer to buy or sell round amounts of Deutsche Marks but be less willing to execute a transaction in dollars which would convert into an odd Deutsche Mark amount. For instance, if the rate in New York was US $0.41 per DM1, the reciprocal would be DM2.439 per US dollar. If the New York bank bought

DM1 000 000 at 0.41, it would be easier to undo the transaction as it is highly likely that there would be buyers of Deutsche Marks in round amounts of 1 000 000 in the New York market. On the other hand, if the German bank expressed a preference to deal in dollars on the German quotation basis the bank might sell $1 000 000 and end up with DM2 439 000. This amount would naturally be less attractive to other New York operators and the bank might have to sell DM2 500 000, in the process taking a short position in Deutsche Marks of DM61 000, not a large position but still a minor nuisance.

Market-makers normally will be more inclined to quote in whatever way the contacting party wishes to be priced, though there is usually a marginal cost involved in asking for a special favour.

Bid and offered side

As is the practice in most markets, foreign exchange rates are quoted with an *offered side* and a *bid side*. The difference between offer and bid is the dealing turn, erroneously referred to as the profit margin. Whether the difference is called a dealing turn or a profit margin, it is infinitesimal, and enormous amounts will have to be turned over to generate adequate profits for the quoting bank. If he quoted prices all day long without moving the bid or offered side the market-maker might transact business only on one side of the rate and at the end of the day find that only selling or only buying has taken place, and a large over-sold or over-bought position in a foreign currency created. That is not the way dealers in the banks will operate. Like traders or brokers in other markets, whether in commodities or on the Stock Exchange, the exchange dealer will move his rates, lay off surplus positions with other traders, go long in one currency and short in another and use averaging techniques, some of which will be detailed in this chapter. The analogy with a bookmaker is fairly accurate, and although few bookmakers have become foreign exchange dealers and vice versa, the basic qualities required are the same. Taking views in foreign currencies is a business of odds and before a dealer will commit his bank the odds will have to be in his favour. When the odds are uncertain a dealer will commit his bank only for a small amount, whichever way he guesses is the least risky.

Competition and rate movements

Some commercial users are nonplussed by the fact that foreign exchange rates can vary from bank to bank, with some being competitive most of the time and others never. They might think that the uncompetitive banks will only do business which is absolutely certain of generating a profit whereas the competitive ones are cleverer or more willing to take a risk, a gamble. The truth of the matter is that banks reflect the basic philosophy of senior management and the interpretation of the dealers. Some banks will be quite satisfied with small profits on volume transactions which build into large profits. Others would rather transact less business but be assured that all of it is profitable. To be competitive, risks have to be taken; they can be large, they can be small, but a bank with an experienced dealing team will find ways of limiting the risks to manageable proportions.

Few banks specializing in foreign exchange can offer expertise in all currencies. Each bank tends to cover a range of major and minor currencies for spot and forward quotations, though some prefer to deal in spot only whilst others deal only in forward markets through hedged (or swap) operations (*see* Chapter 8). In order to find competitive rates commercial users and correspondent banks will have to establish relationships with a number of market-makers; this will enable them to identify the appropriate market-maker when they have to cover. It is obviously advantageous to know the specialist in a difficult currency or maturity.

A quoting bank will very soon prove its competitiveness by the number of times transactions are concluded based on its rates. Naturally, this could also mean that the rates quoted were too competitive and that instead of profits losses are being accumulated and excessive long or short positions being incurred. There may be times when the specialist bank deliberately or by accident quotes outside the market range. For instance, a specialist bank can be ultra-competitive by quoting within the market range, or by offering a better selling or buying rate than is currently being quoted by other banks. By, for example, pricing the selling side better than the going market rate, a bank not only becomes very competitive but can direct the transaction flow one way, in other words ensuring that only buyers of the foreign currency will come forward and transact business. Sometimes a bank may quote a competitive selling rate for one currency and a competitive buying rate for another: the bank wishes to 'go short' of the first currency and 'go long' of the second; the chances are that the first currency is a weak and the second a hard currency. If by taking these quoting postures the bank becomes known as offering a superb foreign exchange service, the purpose of the exercise will have been fulfilled. Also the more business is generated at the right rates, the more information on prevailing market tendencies becomes available to the market-maker, making it much easier for him to 'bend' the rates to suit his book.

How professional foreign exchange dealers operate in the spot market

Normally foreign exchange markets in Europe open at about 8.30–9.00 a.m. and the London market tends to open at about the same time as other European centres, even when the United Kingdom is an hour behind the Continent. The market-maker, and the competition—essential to the functioning of an efficient market —will start the day with relatively moderate currency exposures left over from the previous dealing day. They may be large if there is stability in the market, or if the direction of a particular exchange rate is fairly certain. However, assuming a stable market with stable currencies the positions will probably be moderate. At this stage, we shall concentrate on the spot market and ignore the complexities which forward dealings can have on spot rates.

The market bases its opening quotations usually on the closing rates of a previous time zone, but this quotation will be updated as in Europe most of the major currencies are dealt in by banks established in the countries of those currencies. This makes the European market less volatile than for instance the New York or the Far Eastern market, after Europe has closed down for the day.

Once the market-maker has established quoting rates either by hearing from other operators or by sheer guesswork he will quote his buying and selling rates for currencies he deals in on a professional basis. He will quote these rates to contacts over the telephone and telex and may also 'show' his rates to the brokers.

The market-maker only engages to deal with parties he considers trustworthy and even when he allows the brokers to quote his rates it does not mean that he will accept any name. He must have an established dealing limit approved by his senior management for a name before he can deal. Dealing limits exist to ensure that no settlement exposures are incurred with parties considered unsuitable for this facility. There are cases when a bank refuses to deal with a bank of equal standing because it feels that this is helping the competition, but fortunately this approach is less prevalent these days—what is good for the competition is usually good for the quoting bank as well. To put this differently, they may have opposite interests and thus it may suit them to deal with each other.

Example 4

Our market-maker is resident in Country A and his favourite currency is that of Country B, which he normally quotes indirectly, *i.e.* Cbs against his own unit of account Ca1 . For this example, we will take it for granted that the proven parity between the two currencies is Ca 1 = Cb 2.

To quote the same rate to prospective buyers and sellers alike might generate large volume, but would definitely not be profitable for the quoting bank. At best the sales would match the purchases and at the worst there would be all sales and no purchases or vice versa. This could happen if the rate was a definite improvement on one side of the quotations in the market-place. The practice of quoting one rate good for buying or selling was not unusual before the advent of the floating rate system, but it is not something to be encouraged. In any case, dealers who engage in this kind of egotistical activity rarely stay dealers for very long.

The market-maker—the quoting bank—basing his opening rates on the information obtained from the market and other participants quotes:

$$\text{Ca } 1 = 1.9999\text{—}2.0001$$

The first rate is the selling and the second the buying rate. It is likely that the quotation will then be simplified to 1.9999–01 and even 99–01 as it can be assumed that participants and other market-makers are sufficiently experienced to know what the figures stand for. However, as exchange rates have shown extreme volatility over the last few years, it is more appropriate to state the full rate, although it is not necessary to clarify the 01; this must obviously represent 2.0001, as the buying always follows the selling rate. Professional operators, of course, do not state 'I buy at such and such a rate' unless they only have a one-way interest, in which case they will make this clear by saying 'I am only a buyer at . . .' Our market-maker opened 1.9999–01 because the general market quotes 1.9998–00 (2.0000) and by improving on the selling rate, he feels reasonably sure that buyers of Cbs will use his rates and effect their business with him. He has the edge on the market. On the other hand, if a seller of Cbs happened to like the 2.0001, which seems highly unlikely, he could turn round and sell the Cbs to a market operator at 2.0000 and be sure to make a profit; that is, with the proviso all other things remaining equal.

When the first inquirer contacts the bank and is shown the price 1.9999–01 and this selling side is better than the rest of the market, if the inquirer has an interest in buying Cbs a bargain will be struck. The market-maker in A now has a short position in Cbs and as the currencies have been fairly stable for a long time and it is early in the dealing day, he may adjust his quotation to reflect his interest in buying Cbs to cover the short position. Or, if he so desires, he can continue to quote the competitive selling rate if he wishes to stay short. Assuming he would like to cover the exposure, he can either buy back the Cbs in the open market at 1.9998 or hope that a natural seller will show up at better than 1.9999. To encourage sellers he will no doubt make it interesting for them and improve on the market and quote 1.99975–1.99995, marginally better than the market's buying price of 2.0000. As a matter of interest, the fourth place after the decimal point is referred to as a *point* or *points*, whilst in quotations to five places after the decimal point the fifth place is called a *pip* or *pips*. Beware, however, as pips and points get confused even by the most professional of dealers and it is always wise to establish what is meant by statements such as 'I'll improve by a point (or pip).'

By the dealer quoting 1.99975–995 and the general market being 1.9998–00, the dealer has protected himself from any further buying interests, and he may find discriminating sellers at 1.9995. If the amount of his purchase (or purchases) matches the sum he sold he will have realized a modest profit. However, if someone sells to him an amount in excess of his requirements he can either decline to execute more than his amount, or if he accepts the challenge he will change his quote once again to one where he will get more buyers and few sellers.

In this dealing approach, we have assumed that both banks were resident in Country A and looked at Cbs as being the foreign currency. But the situation would not have changed as long as the contacting party was a seller or buyer of Cbs and wished to be quoted in Cb terms for Cas.

Example 5

If the above transactions had been concluded with a bank or customer resident in Country B, the mechanics would have remained identical but with a different emphasis. The first transaction would probably have been conducted as follows.

Contact in Country B gets in touch with the bank in A by telephone or telex and after the normal introductions asks: 'How do you quote Cas against Cbs?' Answer: '1.9999–01.'

After some hesitation, possibly to check the rates with another bank: 'I sell to you Ca 1 000 000 at 1.9999 value . . .' (making sure that the spot date is the same in A and B). Answer: 'I buy from you Ca 1 000 000 at 1.9999 value . . .'

There is no need to exchange payment instructions as the beneficiaries are resident in the currencies' native countries.

In principle, there is no difference between the approach adopted in Examples 4 and 5. However, in Example 4 both banks looked at Cbs as being the foreign currency, whereas in Example 5 the contacting party considered Cas to be the foreign currency. The dealer in A will have to reverse his thinking quickly, and say to himself 'Buying Cas is like selling Cbs.' Experienced operators do not find this shift of emphasis difficult, particularly if one of the currencies is the national one.

One problem attached to dealing with parties outside the currency area is that when they deal in terms of the market-maker's own currency, it will be difficult to match the foreign currency amount. By buying Ca 1 000 000 from the party in B at 1.9999, a sale of Cb 1 999 900 has been effected, but it is uncertain whether there will be a seller in the market willing to deal in an odd amount, and thus the quoting bank will remain long of Cb 100 when eventually it manages to find a seller(s) of Cb 2 000 000. Most professional banks accept these differences as part of the normal trading 'game', although they may be less inclined to deal on this basis when the foreign currency is a minor one which is not readily dealt in the market place.

Third-country transactions

It is not unusual for a customer or bank in a third country to be interested in the currencies of Country A and Country B. A bank in Country C might have accumulated a short position in Cas and a long one in Cbs. If there is no ready market for these currencies in Country C, the bank can then contact a market-maker in either Country A or in Country B. If there is little to choose between the quoting banks in the two countries, the bank in Country C will try to contact the bank in the country where it can match at least one of the currencies, particularly if it is a round amount, and leave the discrepancy in the currency with the odd amount. It might also be possible that if, let us say, Cb is a reserve currency the difference will be left in this country, unless Country A's currency is considered to be the stronger, in which case all oddments will be accumulated in Cas.

Why an operator in Country C should wish to take positions in Cas versus Cbs is easy to explain. It would be very similar to a London bank which during the dealing day sold French francs against sterling and from another party bought dollars against sterling. By later on doing one deal—that is buying French francs against dollars—the exposure will be cancelled out and may be more profitable especially if the French franc and dollar deals against sterling had been concluded at favourable rates, thus producing an advantageous cross dollar/French franc rate.

Averaging

Banks in their dealings adopt divergent strategies and tactics. Examples 4 and 5 on pp. 90–92 described the activities of a bank

93

which uses tactics, not simply taking a large position, but hoping by juggling the exchange rates to make quick but only modest profits. Banks in countries with few foreign exchange regulations and a history of active foreign exchange relationships may be more adventurous in their views.

Some dealers may be firmly convinced that they have insight into the future of exchange rates and take large, once and for all, positions until their view is proved right and they realize large profits. There are also those who think they have the golden touch in spite of which they realize losses more often than not; they will not last for long. Large positions can be created by doing one or a number of large transactions at one rate or within a narrow range. When some banks make large profits, others may lose. As large transactions tend to unsettle the market they make it necessary for the central banks to intervene, which is not a good thing for the market as a whole or for the reserve situation of a country.

Less ambitious but more skilful dealers will take the view that they cannot with any accuracy predict how market rates will move, or for that matter how far they will move, and will be willing to take only small open positions which reflect their opinions as to where the rates should go. These banks and their dealers will adopt *averaging* postures in moderate amounts. If they feel reasonably sure that, let us say, currency B is bound to depreciate in a floating context, or devalue under a fixed-rate system, they may start selling Cbs in moderate amounts and sell more whenever the rate moves further down, or even up if for some inexplicable reason (usually a technical one) Cbs appreciate in the short term. By selling small amounts at different rate levels, within a range they consider appropriate, they establish a short position at a *melded* rate, and will not be as vulnerable as the once-for-all position-taker.

Example 6

If the market-maker in A took the view that Cbs were due to depreciate against Cas but was uncertain of the timing or the magnitude of the change, he might decide to accumulate over a period of time what he considered an adequate short book in Cbs.

Assuming that the bank in A wished to accomplish this by selling at the going rate an amount of Cbs every day, it might start on Day 1 by selling Cb 1 000 000 at its quoting rate of 1.9999, and the following with another amount at 2.0000 and so on every day for ten days; finding that every day the rate has dropped by one point, at the end of the ten days he will have a short position of Cb 10 000 000 at an average rate of 2.00035. At that point, he could decide to stop, or go on if the rate kept dropping by one point a day. Compared to his melded rate the overall price would improve day by day as his melded rate would worsen by less than the market movement, and if the market stabilized or reversed slightly there might be ample time to 'come out' of the position. By following this strategy the bank does not violently distort the existing rate structure and makes some contribution to the overall market volume. If all the banks adopted the same *modus operandi* Cbs could only weaken, but fortunately few operators take the same decision simultaneously.

Example 6 is a dream version of averaging, which would rarely be put into practice with the arithmetic progression adopted above.

Averaging can be used in either direction. If our market-maker, when the rate for Cbs drops to 2.0010, feels that this is the low point though it could possibly go lower still, he may prefer to start covering the exposure 'on the way down'. In other words, instead of staying a seller he will adopt a buying posture in Cbs, again utilizing the averaging approach, buying in Cb 1 000 000 every day or every time Cbs drop by a further point until it is obvious that Cbs have reached their absolute low. When he feels that Cbs have depreciated too much he may then adopt a buying posture, cover his short position and go long of Cbs until another *resistance level* is reached. Resistance levels can be reached for a number of reasons. The market as a whole may feel that a currency has depreciated by more than is warranted in the circumstances, or profit-taking puts a stop to any further depreciation or appreciation. And profit-taking can take place at any level where market-makers or speculators decide that it is time to realize some of their gains. Naturally, resistance levels are sometimes set by loss-takers as well, but that is rarely the case; loss-takers will tend to influence the exchange rate detrimentally whatever the state of the currency.

Banks which go in for averaging are normally in a better position to quote competitive rates to their customers or correspondents than those who try to 'read' the market, with the proviso that the averaging bank has taken the right view in the first place. In reality, however, it does not matter whether the bank is initially successful or not as long as it is willing to continue with its policy; one of the rates, either the buying or the selling, will be more competitive than the prevailing market rates for the commercial user or the correspondent bank.

Market-making in more than one currency

Not many banks will specialize in only one currency, as this may leave them vulnerable to the vagaries of the market. Most will try to develop expertise in at least two, preferably complementary, currencies, one weak, the other strong. This will enable the market-maker to offset one currency exposure against another, and in most cases they will be short in the weak and long in the strong currency, for obvious reasons.

The more currencies a bank deals in, the more expertise it will require and acquire and the more competitive it can be in its quotation. It is rare, however, that more than at the most two currencies can be dealt in in volume against the national currency. For instance, whilst the US dollar is the main foreign currency in most markets, sterling is usually only dealt against dollars. Consequently there is not a good market for sterling against Deutsche Marks or French francs. A London bank wishing to add another currency apart from dollars against sterling may well have to become expert in, let us say, Deutsche Marks against dollars rather than Deutsche Marks against sterling. To operate efficiently, the bank will then have to take a long-term view and decide to be long (or short) of Deutsche Marks most of the time and short (or long) of dollars, although over the short term it may well operate in the reverse way.

Banks which operate strategic positions will have to be careful when making prices to customers, as the quotation to the customer should not be influenced by the strategic position if this would penalize the end user. Commercial customers should on the whole be given advantageous rates resulting from right dealing decisions and not be made to suffer because of wrong dealing decisions.

To do otherwise might encourage commercial customers to deal with other banks.

Cross-currencies

Exchange rates should always reflect the indirect parities, otherwise arbitrageurs will enter the market and take advantage of the situation. The *indirect parity* is that which can be calculated through at least two other currencies. If Ca 1 = Cb 2 and Cc 1 = 0.40, Ca 1 must equal Cc 5, as Cb 2/0.40 = Cc 5. For Ca 1 to appreciate to Cc 6 or depreciate to Cc 4 would also require commensurate adjustments in Cc 1 = Cb 0.40 to Cc 1 = Cb 0.333 or Cc 1 = Cb 0.50. As it is normal practice in the market to quote buying and selling prices, quoting parties will have to be careful that their prices do not diverge widely from the current parity or equilibrium level. Dealing margins are so small and dealers so well informed that this will rarely happen. In any case, if a quoting bank makes a substantial error when indicating an exchange rate the other party should point out the mistake. A professional or commercial participant who deliberately takes advantage of a pricing mistake should not be surprised if from then on the market-maker will refuse to trade with him.

Example 7

When a bank decides to make a market in two or more currencies, it will have to co-ordinate activities to gain the greatest advantage. However, customers should always be given competitive rates whatever the strategic position or short-term tactics it has adopted.

Quoting the two currencies against its own and assuming that there is good market in both, the bank will open in the morning Ca 1 = Cb 1.9999–01 (2.0001) and Ca 1 = Cc 4.9997–02 (5.0002). The market-maker will sell Cbs at 1.9999 and Ccs at 4.9997 and on the reverse side will be willing to buy the respective currencies at 2.0001 and 5.0002. If the market price for Cbs is 1.9998–00 and for Ccs 4.9998–03, it is clear that our party has taken a deliberate view to go short of Cbs and long of Ccs. The chances are that a buyer of Cbs and a seller of Ccs will come forward eventually and if they happened to execute transactions denominated in equal amounts of Cas the bank might find itself short of the equivalent of Ca 1 000 000 at 1.9999 = Cb 1 999 900 and long of Cc 5 000 200. As the Cas match exactly, the exposure incurred is that of Cbs against Cbs at a cross-rate of 5.0002/1.9999 = 2.500225, as Cbs are quoted in Country C, or 1.9999/5.0002 = 0.399964, the reciprocal rate quoted in Country B for Ccs.

By selling Cbs and buying Ccs the bank has incurred an exposure in two currencies without involvement of the national currency. From now on the quoter can make a price in Cbs against Ccs and as the rate amounted to 2.500225 the bank has to find out whether this is a rate which can be readily used in the open market. The *indirect parities* for Cbs against Ccs can be worked out by calculating that if first Cbs had to be bought against Cas at 1.9998, and Ccs sold at 5.0003, the selling rate in Country C for Cbs has to be approximately 5.0003/ 1.9998 = 2.5004 and the buying rate 4.9997/2.0000 = 2.49985, and that banks in Country C making markets in Cbs would quote approximately 2.49985–2.5004. As the Cbs were sold at 2.500225, by buying them back from a bank in Country C at 2.5004, a loss would be realized. If the market-maker in Country A feels that among his contacts there are some who may wish to transact business in Cbs against Ccs, he will retain the position and possibly quote 2.49995–2.5005, improving on the general market price. There is also the possibility that he may prefer to remain short of Cbs against Ccs, as he feels that Cbs will weaken, or conversely Ccs strengthen, sooner rather than later which, of course, would be reflected in a more favourable exchange rate and a clear profit on the long Ccs position when it is undone.

Stable markets

In the days of the Bretton Woods system, banks could take views in foreign currencies almost with impunity. Under the fixed-rate system the most a speculator could lose was 1.5 per cent, but he would have had to be very unfortunate to have dealt at either extreme of the intervention levels. Floating rates by nature reflect unstable markets, and the risks are magnified. However, this should not stop a bank from taking views; the amounts will simply have to be smaller in comparison to those that could be dealt in under a narrow fixed-rate system. Under the Bretton Woods system, a bank might have transacted and taken positions in amounts of $5 000 000 with the maximum loss being 1.5 per cent and with the knowledge that exchange rates would very seldom move by more than 2 per cent in a day; the bank could take positions of $1–2 million without incurring a greater exposure. Amounts can be increased or decreased depending on the stability of the market.

Indication rates

Commercial market users frequently mistake a dealer's qualification of an exchange rate 'I indicate 1.9999–01' to mean that the dealer is willing to deal at these rates, whereas the dealer wishes to tell the contacting party either that he has finished dealing for the day or that the market is too uncertain and that he would rather not deal. To overcome this problem, it might be advisable for dealers to qualify rates which are given for information only by stating this fact clearly: 'These rates are for information only', and to make sure that the other party understands and is given an explanation. This is better than leaving the contacting party with the mistaken impression that the bank has stopped dealing altogether or is not interested in the transaction.

When other expressions are used which confuse the 'outsider' the dealer should also be asked to clarify; this might help him to be more discriminating in his use of jargon, especially when talking to a non-professional.

Hints to commercial users

The large multi-national will usually be given preferential treatment by the banks because the overall relationship is so important. Medium-sized and small companies tend to be served with some reluctance by the banks for a number of reasons. The amounts transacted may be rather small and thus costly to handle, and the currencies may not always be covered in depth by the customers' sole bankers. Medium-sized companies in good financial condition may be able to overcome this problem by changing their bank or using a more professional dealer for their foreign exchange requirements, but for the small company there is very little that can be done apart from pestering their bankers to become more efficient.

If banks are hesitant to quote for small amounts, or even refuse to quote at all for the business, it should not surprise the interested party. The cost of handling a foreign exchange transaction varies from bank to bank, though if all expenses in 1977 were added up each individual transaction would be found to have cost in sterling from £10 and in US dollars from $25 upwards. Thus, before a transaction becomes profitable, a bank has to make at least this difference. Costs will reflect salaries, equipment (as banks have more and more to invest in computers and software), rental of telex lines, etc. Small companies with imports and exports denominated in foreign currencies can try to overcome this problem by buying and selling in larger amounts and by effecting payment by cheque rather than telegraphic transfer so long as their suppliers, for instance, do not demand payment in a more direct and quicker fashion. The company may then have to decide whether its import or export business in small quantities is likely to expand or become more profitable; if this seems unlikely, it may have to go in for a more remunerative business. The same conditions would apply to unprofitable domestic business. No company can continue to lose money. Such management decisions, though unpleasant, are often necessary.

In countries like the United Kingdom, foreign exchange regulations may inhibit hedging and covering operations which cannot be substantiated in documentary form because no invoices or import documents can be produced. This is the side effect of regulations which protect the currency whilst simultaneously creating difficulties for genuine business transactions. Long term, the only solution lies in the removal of the regulations by devaluing the currency by more than is required, thus ensuring that no further outflows will occur. The speculator will hesitate to sell a currency which is obviously under-valued, though he may not be so inclined if it is over-valued.

The spot market should be used only by the banks and the large companies which can interpret short-term trends and have sufficient influence to get the market-makers to quote rates whatever the market conditions prevailing at the time. Small and medium-sized companies should endeavour to cover their exposures in the forward market, if not immediately the exposure becomes apparent then certainly well before the time that payments or receipts are due.

Companies with numerous in- and outflows in different currencies, so long as these cover a broad range of weak and strong, are in the strongest position. They can take the view that as short positions in weak currencies roughly match long positions in strong ones there is then no need to cover the risks; what they will lose on the swings they will recoup on the roundabouts.

Pricing of imports and exports

It may be appropriate to point out again that spot exchange rates are not the rates to use to fix the price for an import or export. This applies even when the national currency is used to establish a contract. Spot exchange rates reflect only the immediate value of a currency, whereas forward rates denote the value of a currency at the future date that an invoice will have to be settled, and forward cover can be taken out to ensure that the price of the import or export is immutably fixed.

All parties interested in international trade—financial executives, marketing men and production managers—should be aware that to establish the effective price of an import or export the forward rate for a currency is the one to be used. Between the time a transaction involving the movement of most goods or services is negotiated, and the effective payment date, periods of three to six months will elapse and if the merchant wishes to cover the currency risk immediately he will have to take out a *forward contract*.

8. Forward exchange rates

The choice of spot or forward rate

Experts tend to disagree about the effect that forward rates actually have on the exchange or spot rates of a currency. Is it favourable? Or does the forward rate influence the eventual value of a currency unduly? The discussion is rather academic and should not affect the decisions which have to be made by a company treasurer. If the company treasurer has to cover a risk in the forward market to ensure price-effectiveness, and definitely if inclusive of the forward cost or profit the price is still competitive he has no choice; he should cover. Unless his company is widely dispersed over the world, and cash management programmes which cancel out exchange exposures can be operated, a real profit is always preferable to a situation which with luck may turn out to be more profitable but which may also turn out not to be so.

It is generally accepted that in normal circumstances, and if there are no inhibiting constraints on the movement of money, the *forward margin* is the difference between the interest rates operating in two or more countries. These forward margins should reflect the interest differentials, or interest parities.

Before the Second World War, the forward rates between sterling and US dollar would have been based on the respective Treasury Bill rates. A Treasury Bill rate of 3 per cent in the United States and 4 per cent in the United Kingdom would have resulted in a forward premium for dollars of 1 per cent especially with three months' maturity. And a 1 per cent per annum difference would mean an effective $\frac{1}{4}$ per cent difference between the spot dollar price and the three months outright price.

Nowadays, it is necessary to note that forward margins are dictated by *effective interest rate differentials*. For most currencies, the effective interest differential is not obtainable in the domestic money markets but in the Euro-markets. Internal and effective international rates can vary substantially. It is not unusual for external or Euro-sterling, Euro-French francs and lire to command interest rates several per cent higher than those obtainable in the domestic markets of the respective countries. These interest differentials in the effective markets are not caused so much by domestic rates, although these do exert an influence, but more by speculative pressures in the exchange markets.

However, as explained previously, as international trade is rarely conducted on the basis of immediate settlement these forward rates will in fact dictate the effective price of a product.

Why forward margins? Why interest differentials?

In a static market, forward margins will equal the interest differentials, and these interest differentials will be close to those prevailing in the domestic markets. However, when a crisis arises the speculators and genuinely interested parties will sell the suspect currency either before the receipts are due or, when it is a case of pure speculation, without possessing any assets in the currency. If these selling pressures affected only the spot a number of operators would have to go short of the spot currency, but as it is highly unlikely that these operators will have overdraft or other credit facilities, they will have to cover the short positions somehow. The only way the position can be covered is by either buying back the currency for spot, or by borrowing the currency from a party willing to place funds. Banks are in a favourable position as among their contacts they may find a customer or another bank willing to place the currency on deposit with them for one day or longer. Non-banks will find it difficult to borrow the funds and may have to buy the currency for spot and simultaneously sell it for another maturity, thus establishing a forward position. The demand for the currency will not strengthen the spot exchange rate but will cause an increase in the interest rate speculators are willing to pay in order to cover their short positions. The swap transactions of the professional banks involve buying for a near date and selling for a date in the future; even if only for the day after spot, these activities will further influence the effective interest rate in the international market.

Why there should be interest differentials between the international and the domestic markets is another subject, although one closely connected with foreign exchange. Suffice it to say that exchange regulations on in- and outflows, taxation, reserve requirements and other inhibiting factors will usually keep domestic rates lower than those in the uncontrolled Euro-markets. The Euro-markets consist of many more participants than the domestic equivalents. For instance, there are more banks and organizations actively trading in the Euro-sterling market than in the London money market. Obviously, most of the time, the volume in domestic sterling on a day-to-day basis will exceed that transacted in Euro-sterling. But to some extent the greater volume reflects only the larger number of small payments which pass to and fro within the domestic clearing system.

Forwards and the commercial user

Before analysing the intricacies of the forward exchanges it might be advisable to point out some of the advantages and the drawbacks the forward market presents to the commercial user.

Example 8

Let us go back to Example 4, page 90, the market-making bank which quoted spot Cb 1.9999–01, and add to this quotation the further complication of the interest differential. In Country A interest rates (and for simplicity we shall assume that there are no external rates, as domestic funds can flow freely in and out of the country) are for most periods in the region of 4 per cent, whilst in Country B the equivalent interest rates are about 5 per cent, a 1 per cent per annum clear differential. Bank A will not require detailed knowledge of other market-makers' forward rates, as for example in the three months period the forward margin has to be approximately 1 per cent. One per cent of Cb 2.00 = 0.02 and the three months rate must be somewhere around Cb 0.02/4 = 0.0050. To be really accurate, we should have divided 0.02 by 365 and multiplied the result by the exact number of days for three months, *i.e.* 0.02/365 × 91 = 0.004986, still close enough to 0.0050 for quotation purposes; however, on a wider margin, *e.g.* 0.20 (10 per cent per annum), the exact number of days would have had quite an effect on the rate, as $0.2 \times 91/365 = 0.04986$, a difference of 1.4 points or 14 pips.

Forwards are always quoted as margins, and few banks will automatically convert the forward rates into outright prices when contacted, unless requested to do so by the other party.

If a party requested Bank A for the spot and forward (three months), the bank might quote:

spot Cb 1.9999–2.0001 (1.9999–01)
three months Cb 0.0051–0.0049 (usually quoted as 51–49)

and thus the outright rate at which the bank would be selling Cbs is 1.9948, and conversely it would buy Cbs at 1.9952. As spreads are applied to spot and forward quotations, forward outright rates will be wider than the buying and selling margins for spot transactions.

Because of the interest differential, forward Cbs are at a premium; in other words more Cas will have to be expended to obtain the same amount of Cbs for delivery in three months than would have to be paid for an equivalent amount of Cbs on the spot.

The longer the period, the more the forward rates will widen and consequently the greater the spread between buying and selling rates. Normally this holds true, though during a major currency crisis there are times when shorter maturities may command wider spreads than the longer ones. This is caused by the greater demand for or supply of immediate funds where the greatest shortage or availability exists. Another reason for the longer dates showing wider margins is that the longer the period the fewer specialists will actively trade in the maturities and thus the few banks in a position to execute orders have to take greater risks as well. The limits which banks set for each other also affect the issue, as the longer the period the longer the two banks may not be able to deal with each other, or at least not to the extent they might wish to do. Some banks also restrict their dealing activities to periods which they find the most profitable and the least risky. For some, that may mean up to three months, for others six and for many more maximum periods of one year. This can create problems for exporters and importers of capital goods denominated in foreign currencies. Fortunately in several countries export guarantee organizations will cover this kind of exposure and thus minimize the risks.

Anything which diverges from the norm will usually cost more, or cut into the profits. Importers or exporters who wish to cover themselves for what is called an 'odd' maturity or 'odd' date, may find fewer banks willing to quote and consequently the rates will be less competitive than those for the normal calendar periods of one, three and six months. This is easy to understand, as banks cannot cover themselves in the market for dates which do not form part of the normal maturity structure at the time, and this can also apply to periods which are not adequately covered by market-makers. For instance, in French francs there is usually a good market up to six months, and even for one year, but there are times when it will be difficult to buy or sell French francs for nine months. This is not an odd date, just an odd period; for a bank to execute the customer's order it will have to incur a 'gap' exposure, *e.g.* buy French francs for delivery in nine months and be forced to sell French francs for either six months or one year, thus incurring a gap exposure of six to nine, or nine to twelve, months.

Commercial interests may not be able to develop the dealing sense which is instinctive to the dealer, but they should and must acquire a knowledge of the techniques which are employed by the dealing fraternity, particularly in the forward market. To achieve a thorough knowledge, it is necessary to study dealers' ploys and thinking.

We shall now consider some of the positions taken by dealers, and the way in which they will interpret interest and margin movements should assist to clarify the problem. Dealers are in a favourable position; they can take positions and when they prove to be wrong reverse them at the drop of a hat. The commercial treasurer must make a once-for-all decision and consequently should as much as possible try to protect himself from the outset against any unfavourable development.

Forwards in an unstable exchange market

In an unstable spot market, the forward margins and spreads will widen because there will be fewer buyers or sellers, and it is quite possible that the one-way market phenomenon will be in operation in the spot market. Dealers are sometimes requested to explain to non-professionals why rates are then so wide or only obtainable on one side of the market and will quite often respond to this type of inquiry in an off-hand manner: 'The exchange rate is weak because there are more buyers than sellers.' This of course is a very unsatisfactory answer for a company treasurer who has to justify an exchange decision to his senior management.

This situation, when it prevails in an unstable exchange market, can be compared to the reaction which takes place in a Stock Exchange when extremely good or bad news brings about the need for a major adjustment in the price of a share. Naturally extremely bad news is more difficult to interpret than good news. Initially the jobbers in the case of depressing news will react by widening the difference between their buying and selling prices and will be inclined to make their selling price more attractive than the buying price. They will continue to adjust the price structure until buyers come forward to bring prices into balance. At a certain point they may feel that the price has gone too low and this may encourage the jobbers to buy some shares for their own account. Not surprisingly, when a company goes bankrupt that is the end of the share quotation for market purposes.

Countries do not go bankrupt in the same way as commercial companies. They are in a better position to improve on a given situation by economic and monetary decisions; for one thing they can devalue or depreciate the national currency, although quite often that is the last option available to them. As we have seen earlier, governments are not inclined to take actions which visibly demonstrate mismanagement of the national economy. The foreign exchange markets tend, however, to take the view that the currency price must be adjusted sooner or later and will become hesitant to buy the currency in these circumstances.

The forward market will show a currency's unpopularity almost immediately if there is fixed exchange rate system in operation. Under floating rates, the spot rate will be very volatile as well but since the central bank may try to keep an orderly market it will still be the forward rates which will take the brunt of the pressure.

Forward rates in these circumstances may in percentage terms widen by a larger margin than is justified in the light of the probable percentage of an exchange rate adjustment. The widening of the forwards will reflect the anticipated change of the currency as well as the necessity for speculators and genuine hedgers with short positions to extend their positions for a future date. The very short-term periods will then be particularly susceptible to widening margins as the longer dates may already be wider than the expected rate change.

The *static theory* of forward exchanges, now discounted by most experts, held that the forward price of a currency had to be the same as the spot rate unless market operators felt that the currency would change its parity at some time in the future. The operators would then by the market process, that is by buying and selling the currency forward, establish the rate at which they felt the currency should be valued. Nowadays, it is generally accepted that the interest parities are all-important, and though in times of stress the forward rates may for short periods of time not be in line with the existing interest rates it may well be that this is only the case because the interest rates have some catching up to do.

The Interest Parity Theory on the whole will apply solely to the major currencies. The forwards of minor currencies are less influenced by the interest rates, as the volume of forward dealing will greatly exceed that of the deposit markets during crisis periods. This situation can make it simpler for the monetary authorities of a small country to make it difficult, if not impossible, for outsiders to speculate in their currencies.

Swaps

The forward markets operate efficiently because they are based on the simultaneous buying and selling of similar amounts of the same currency for different maturities. By adopting this approach the forward markets can set forward prices without incurring outright exchange risks. The risk that is incurred is that the forward margins will widen or narrow contrary to expectation. In principle, though not in practice, the exchange rate is of lesser importance in the forward market.

For instance, if a bank buys $1 000 000 for spot value, and at the same time sells $1 000 000 forward for delivery in three months' time, it has executed a *swap transaction*. It may well be that the counterparties to the two deals are different banks or even custo-mers, but as long as the amounts are roughly equal a swap has been created. Though normally speaking a swap will be established by placing an order and ensuring that both the selling and buying transactions occur simultaneously, it is not absolutely necessary for this to happen. Swaps can be the result of independent trans-actions. If a customer sells $1 000 000 to the market-maker for spot and a little later another customer or bank buys $1 000 000 for three months, the market-maker can also look at these transactions as constituting a swap, as there is no exchange rate exposure left. The exposure is now that of the forward margins and in stable conditions only the interest differentials will dictate that when the swap transaction is unwound there is a resultant loss or profit.

Example 9

Applying the rates of Example 8, page 104:

$$\text{when the spot rate} = 1.9999\text{--}2.0001$$
$$\text{and the three months} = \quad 51\text{--} \quad 49$$
$$\text{the outright rate for three months} = 1.9948\text{--}1.9952.$$
$$\text{The swap rates for three months then} = \quad 51\text{--} \quad 49.$$

Outright prices would be used only for buying and selling cur-rencies with commercial customers and banks which are not specialized in foreign exchange or in the particular currency in which the market-maker operates and specializes.

The market-makers in forward transactions operate the simul-taneous buying and selling approach because this allows them to concentrate on the important aspect of the forward rates, the interest differentials. Naturally the strength or weakness of an exchange rate in a crisis situation will have an effect on the swap rate, but this can be handled by adjusting the forward rates whenever a crisis is imminent. By not taking outright exposures the forward market-makers are more flexible in their approach. The forward market, although in total volume larger than the spot market, is divided over a number of maturities: one, two, three, six (nine) months, one year. The longer the period and the more exotic the currency the fewer are the market-makers and the fewer the possibilities to reverse an unwanted spot against forward position. If the operators had to concern themselves with both the exchange rate and the interest rate exposures this would inhibit their freedom to operate and slow down the whole quoting process.

Involuntary swaps, as referred to on p. 109, are incurred mainly as a result of customer activities.

Example 10

If Bank A had quoted the spot and forward rates of Example 9 and a customer had bought three months Cbs outright at 1.9948 rather than try to find another seller of outright Cbs, the bank in Country A would have bought spot Cbs to cover at least the exchange exposure. If this had been accomplished at a rate of 1.9999 the bank would have established a spot against three months swap at a difference of 51 points, which could be undone in the market at no cost. Of course, if the bank was active in the spot exchanges as well, it could have retained the open position in the three months and waited until a natural spot seller of Cbs at 2.0001 showed up. Assuming that the spot and forward amounts were still the same, the bank would then have a more advantageous swap, 2.0001 − 1.9948 = 53 points, and with a general market quotation of 51 for the three months maturity the bank could make a profit by simply reversing the swap. Banks which specialize both in spot and forward in the same currency or currencies place themselves in a much stronger position than those which concentrate on one aspect only. Furthermore, if the bank eventually found another market-maker with a quotation of 50–48 instead of 51–49, the bank might realize a 3 points' profit instead of the original break-even situations.

We mentioned on p. 108 that though in principle the exchange rate does not influence the forward margin, in practice the use of the spot rate will affect the funds immediately available to both parties to a swap transaction.

When a market-maker quotes a spot and forward rate and these are used for a swap transaction, it is customary to use the buying or selling rate depending on whether the spot side is respectively a sale or a purchase. Using spot and forward 1.9999–2.0001 and 51–49, if a bank contacted the market-maker in Country A and suggested a transaction by which the market-maker bought spot Cb 1 000 000 and sold the same amount for three months, it would be 2.0001 that would be used for the spot and 1.9950 (2.0001−51) for the three months. Sometimes contacts will request the use of a rate which facilitates the spot calculation, or the market-maker may even suggest an easier spot rate. In this instance the transaction will result, if Bank A agreed to a rate of Cb 2.00 as a basis for the spot transaction, in more Cas having to be paid on the spot. Dealers will have to be careful not to adjust the spot rate too much because if they agreed to the same principle for buying and selling they might use up more of their own funds:

$$\text{Cb 1 000 000 at 2.0001} = \text{Ca 499 975}$$
$$\text{Cb 1 000 000 at 2.0000} = \text{Ca 500 000}$$

Only a marginal difference, but by agreeing to a rate of 2.0000 Bank B will have to pay an extra Ca 25 to acquire the same amount of Cbs. If the market adopted an approach which automatically used the middle rate of the spot market, this would be fairer to both sides, though in certain conditions it might be difficult to establish the true middle rate. Whatever rate is used, dealers should take into account the extra funds generated or wasted on a transaction.

Premiums and discounts

Forward margins are referred to as *premiums* or *discounts*. When US dollars are at a premium in the United Kingdom, the pound sterling is obviously at a discount in the United States. One man's premium is another man's discount.

Particular care has to be exercised when discussing forward rates in technical terms with parties abroad, as terms such as premium and discount can be confusing, especially when the forward rates are close to the spot rate, and sometimes the forward rates can be premiums on the selling and discounts on the buying side. The problem can be magnified when two parties discuss currencies which are alien to both. A German discussing forward Swiss francs against dollars with a contact in Britain will have to clarify which currency he considers the foreign one. These days it would be advisable to consider dollars as the base currency in all markets, in view of the predominance of this currency in the international money markets. When a German talks to a party in London about the dollar against sterling, he should not refer to the pound as being at a discount or premium as this will confound the British party, since to him sterling is not a foreign currency.

The principle of premiums and discounts is the same whether a system of direct or indirect quotations is in operation. Some slight adjustment in thinking may be required, but that should not prove difficult for those regularly involved in exchange transactions.

Looking at the prices of a centre which applies indirect quotations, premiums and discounts are expressed as follows:

Example 11

	Cbs at premium	*Cbs at discount*
spot	1.9999–2.0001	1.9999–2.0001
three months	51– 49	49– 51
outright	1.9948–1.9952	2.0048–2.0052

The left-hand column shows a currency which is at a premium in the forward markets, whereas the right-hand column shows a currency which is at a discount. Another way of looking at the forward margins is simply to say that where the larger number precedes the smaller it is at a premium and the forward margin has to be deducted from the spot, and where the smaller number precedes the larger it is at a discount, in which case the forward margins are added to the respective spot rates.

In a centre which operates the direct quotation approach, the interpretation is just the same:

Example 12

	Cbs as quoted in Country C	
	Cbs at discount	*Cbs at premium*
spot	2.5000–2.5005	2.5000–2.5005
three months	66– 61	61– 66
outright	2.4934–2.4944	2.5061–2.5071

Though the quotations are direct, the principle remains the same; fewer Ccs will have to be expended in the forwards to buy the same amount of Cbs, thus forward Cbs are at a discount, whereas in the second set of figures the Cbs are at a premium as more Ccs will have to be dispensed to buy forward Cbs. 'Buy high, sell low' is the adage to apply to indirect operations, while direct operations abide by 'Sell high, buy low.'

Confusion can arise over premiums and discounts of third currencies. In London, for instance, the Deutsche Mark is always considered the foreign currency and if the first two columns of Example 12 represented in a rough and ready fashion Deutsche Marks against dollars the London market would consider the first two columns to be the value of the Deutsche Mark rather than that of the dollar and would say that the forward Mark was at a premium against the dollar. It is a question of which currency is considered the base or home currency, and in London, given the importance of the Euro-dollar market, the dollar ranks equal with sterling with the exception of the dollar/sterling rate.

As was mentioned on p. 111, problems can arise when the forward rates are either side of par:

Example 13

When the spot rate	=	1.9999–2.0001
and the three months	=	−1− +1
outright rate	=	1.9998–2.0002

It is necessary to put the minus and plus signs in front of the forward quotations, as otherwise misunderstandings could arise with forward quotations around par. One can assume that the effective interest rates for both currencies must be in equilibrium.

With indirect quotations, premiums indicate that the home currency enjoys higher interest rates than the quoted currency, and discounts reflect higher rates for the quoted currency than for the home currency.

Discounts in direct quotations involve higher interest rates for the currency which is valued in the home currency; *e.g.* when the dollar is at a discount against the Deutsche Mark, the forward margin as quoted in Frankfurt will be deducted and this could only mean that effective interest rates for dollars must be higher than those for Deutsche Marks. On the other hand, premiums would show that higher yields are obtainable for Deutsche Marks than for dollars. Although it may be repetitive, it should be pointed out that, when the dollar is at a discount in Frankfurt, the Deutsche Mark is at a premium in New York.

Forwards and interest rates

As was stated on p. 88, professional operators specialize in aspects of the foreign exchanges which they feel will bring the greatest benefit to their banks. However, as the forward price for a currency is really the true rate to be applied to commercial transactions, unless the bank is expert both in the spot market currency and the forwards for that currency, the customer will not obtain the service he deserves.

Just as for spot positions, professional operators feel that it is not necessary to cover every risk and every exposure immediately. The view they take is that they should be in a position to anticipate risks and changes well before they take place. And should something unforeseen happen they will have to take evasive action very quickly. Averaging in small amounts seems an appropriate means of ensuring that the size of an exposed forward position is never so large that it will endanger the bank. The mere fact that a series of forward rates have been used when building up the spot against forward positions means that the dealer may lose, but the loss, however unpleasant, should be of acceptable proportions.

The series of differing maturities for both purchases and sales is referred to as a dealer's *forward book*. In static markets the profits or losses made on the forward positions will be small, if not insignificant, unless the bank has a large number of customers and correspondent banks with genuine business to transact. A good forward dealer will keep one eye on the effective interest rates for the currencies in which he operates a book, and the other on the possibility of major or minor currency crises. If his book is based on Cbs against Cas, he is well aware that apart from the spot exchange rates there are four factors which may affect the forward margins: interest rates for Cas can go up or come down and the same thing could happen to Cbs. As long as Cas and Cbs go up or down by the same margin at the same time the forward rates should not change. However, if for some reason Cas went up and Cbs down or vice versa this would change the forward margins quite dramatically. Thus it is all-important that any change, or possibility of change, in the interest rate structure should be monitored regularly. Naturally forward rates reflect the market's expectations. Should the market anticipate a change in the interest differential in three months' time the forward margins for maturities in excess of three months will manifest this expected change. It may be that the full extent of the possible change will not be reflected in the forward/forward market, but the tendency will be shown clearly. In a static market with no change expected for the ensuing year currencies A and B, given an interest differential of 1 per cent per annum might be quoted as follows:

Example 14

spot	1.9999–2.0001	
one month	18–	16
three months	51–	49
six months	102–	99
one year	202–	198 (wider spread, longer period)

In this example, the one-month rate seems to be slightly higher than those for the other periods as, converted to an annual basis, 18 × 12 = 216, 16 × 12 = 192. The buying side of the one-month margin is nearer to the full one-year quotation as well as the other maturities than the selling side. This is not unusual, as the shorter the period the more activity will take place and the more immediate pressures of supply and demand will be reflected. The longer periods are dominated by genuine commercial needs, technical posturing of the market-makers and also interest arbitrage situations. And even if arbitrage situations as such do not exist, holders of minor currencies may swap them into one of the major ones such as dollars or sterling as it is considerably easier to find a creditworthy borrower in these at a suitable interest rate.

Forward quotations for periods in excess of one year are obtainable, sometimes for up to five years, in some but not all the major currencies.

However, users of the long-term market should ascertain before making any commitment that prices are being quoted for these longer spans. Naturally there are times, especially during crisis periods, when the long-term segment of the forward market dries up completely.

Using the rates quoted above, a market-maker who takes the view that the one-year swap on the buying side is a good deal may improve on the market rate and quote 204–200, or less aggressively 203–199, to attract a seller of forward Cbs. If the market-maker succeeded in buying forward against the sale of spot Cbs he would have established the desired gap position. If we assume that the cost had been based on the rate of 200, the average margin per month would work out to 200/12 = 16.67 points, putting the market-maker in a more competitive situation than the general market for one-month quotations. By quoting 17.5–15.5 and continuing to do so for the rest of the year he could have 'picked up' 17.5 × 12 = 210 points against an outlay of 200: with the market quoting 18.16, his forward selling rate is more competitive. Not a great profit, but if in the process he has satisfied customers and correspondent banks they may recompense him by leaving balances or engaging in other more profitable business. Let us take it for granted that the market-maker is firmly convinced that interest rates in Country A are bound to go up, and in Country B down; if he is proved right, he will have generated a nice profit margin. If before the transaction was executed the rate in A was 5 per cent and in B 4 per cent and immediately afterwards the rates changed to $5\frac{1}{2}$ per cent and $3\frac{1}{2}$ per cent respectively, the one-year rate would adjust to approximately 402–398. Possibly the spread between buying and selling in this case will widen to 8 or more points. If this happened immediately after the purchase of one-year Cbs against spot, the operator would make a clear profit of 398–200 = 198 points. If the market-maker felt that the difference might widen further still, he might even decide to hold the position and take profits only in the shorter periods of one to three months. As the one-month rate would very likely have changed to something like 36–32, he could realize 32 × 12 = 384 points in the open market, slightly less than taking the immediate one-year profit of 398. This might in fact make him more competitive in his quotations to contacts, and greater benefits could accrue if the interest differentials increased further still. It would be a rare circumstance that interest rates moved in a favourable direction immediately after taking a view or position, but it does happen from time to time. Forward specialists are more exposed, and at the same time less so. As positions are taken for long durations, an exposed posture which seems wrong at first may turn out to be right, quite often for the wrong reasons. Spot dealers are less fortunate in that they have to realize losses and profits that much sooner.

Banks which run books in forwards will in most cases cover two currencies at least, and may well take opposite views in them.

There are two schools of thought in the foreign exchange markets; the first prefers to deal only in the spot exchanges whilst the second tends to cover both spot and forward. In between these extremes there are those who concentrate on one or the other aspect, and on odd-date maturities (that is maturities which do not conform to the market standards of one, two, three, etc., calendar months, *e.g.* one week, two weeks, dates which fall in between the standard value dates, and so on). It is the variety of interests which makes the market comprehensive, as no one bank could cover in depth all currencies, cross-rates, standard forwards and odd dates.

Value dates

The forward value dates of standard maturities are dictated in the first place by the spot date. Most money centres apply the calendar month approach rather than the exact number of days approach followed in some money markets.

The procedure for fixing the value date for a forward transaction is relatively simple. If the spot date falls on the 5th, 6th or any other date in a month, the one-month maturity date will fall on the same date in the following calendar month—on 5th, etc., if it is a business day as described in Chapter 7. If it is not, then it will fall on the first following business day.

The only times that this principle does not operate is when the spot date falls on the last working day of the month and when the spot date falls on a day numerically in excess of the working days in the calendar month of the appropriate period.

Example 15

On transaction date Thursday, 24th February 1977, with a spot date of 28th February 1977 (the last working day) the major dealing periods up to one year showed the following value dates:

one month   31st March 1977
two months   29th April 1977 (30th Saturday)
three months   31st May 1977
four months   30th June 1977
five months   29th July 1977 (30th Saturday, 31st Sunday)
six months   31st August 1977

nine months   30th November 1977
one year   28th February 1978.

These were the value dates applied for dollars against sterling, and maturity dates for other currencies against sterling or cross-rates might have produced earlier last working days in accordance with the principle that no value date should fall into the next calendar month.

To ensure that the eventual outcome of a forward transaction will not cause an unpleasant surprise, it is as well for the inquirer to state his interest very clearly inclusive of the exact value date, even if he is fully aware that the one, two or more months' forward maturity falls on a specific day. And, more important still, when a deal has been consummated the two parties should confirm the whole transaction in detail as follows: 'I (we) buy from you (currency) at (rate) for value (date) . . ., both for the spot side and the forward date of a swap . . .' Though it may seem clever and professional to take some things including the expertise of the counterparty for granted, in practice it leads only to careless and costly mistakes. Accuracy, as has been said before, is absolutely essential when it comes to confirming the details of a transaction.

Interest arbitrage

Although of little interest to most commercial users of the exchange markets, the impact of interest arbitrage can never be ignored. Interest arbitrage activities make greater impact on the major than on the minor or exotic currencies. Whilst for the major currencies in- and outflows of interest arbitrage transactions will originate both domestically and outside the country, the minor currencies are affected mainly by the activities of domestic operators. If forward transactions which involve the movement of funds outside the domestic market are to obtain higher yields, one of the requirements is that foreign exchange regulations and taxation on interest earnings are non-existent or at least can be compensated for in other ways.

There are times when forward transactions are engendered by loans denominated in currencies which are easier to handle in the exchange than in the deposit markets. For instance, international loans made in Belgian francs or guilders will usually be financed out of Euro-dollars, and to accomplish this the lender will have to obtain dollar deposits and then swap the dollars into Belgian francs, thus making it possible to pay Belgian francs to the borrower.

In principle, the interest arbitrage operation is similar to a normal swap transaction, but the interest element will have to be taken into account, otherwise what may seem to be a situation of profit may well turn into one of loss.

Example 16

Bank A established in Country A has the option to take a deposit in Cbs for one year at 4 per cent per annum, or it can swap Cas into Cbs for one year to finance a loan made in Cbs at 4 per cent plus a profit margin. We will assume that the cost of Cas for one year is 5 per cent per annum, that the spot rate is 2.00 and that the one-year rate is 1.98. The longer the period of the swap the more likely it is that the forward rate will not be exact in relation to the interest parity, though the difference will be small.

The amount of the loan is Cb 2 000 000, and as the interest is calculated on the basis of a 360-day year there is a small benefit by obtaining an extra 5 days' interest, *i.e.* 365 days/360. In Country A, as is the custom in the United Kingdom, interest is calculated on the exact year—365 days/365.

Bank A would execute a swap:

$$
\begin{array}{llll}
\text{buy} & \text{spot} & \text{Cb 2 000 000 at 2.00} & = \text{Ca 1 000 000} \\
\text{sell one year} & \text{Cb 2 000 000 at 1.98} & = \text{Ca 1 010 101.01} \\
\hline
& & \text{NIL} & \text{gain Ca} \quad 10\ 101.01
\end{array}
$$

The forward sale shows a gain because more Cas will be received at maturity than have been expended to buy the spot amount.

The effective interest rate on the transaction is:

$$\frac{\text{Ca 10 101.01} \times 100}{1\ 000\ 000} = 1.010101 \text{ per cent per annum}$$

An easy way of checking this instead of going through the whole interest calculation is to establish (in this case) the premium by deducting the forward rate from the spot, *i.e.* 2.00 — 1.98 = 0.02 and

$$\frac{0.02 \times 100}{1.98 \text{ (forward rate)}} = 1.010101 \text{ per cent per annum.}$$

Ignoring the profit margin, which should be realized in any case, the operator uses the base rate of 4 per cent and calculates:

$$\frac{\text{Cb 2 000 000} \times 4 \times 365}{360 \times 100} = \text{Cb 81 111.11.}$$

As the profit will have to be converted into Cas, we assume that the interest amount Cb 81 111.11 is sold at 1.98 in the forward market, thus making sure that on the repayment day of the loan the whole transaction is reflected in the unit of account of Bank A, *i.e.* Cas.

Cb 81 111.11/1.98 = Cas 40 965.21, total interest and swap yield (before profit margin on loan) amounts to Ca 10 101.01 (swap) plus Ca 40 965.21 (interest) = Ca 51 066.22, which equals 5.106622 per cent per annum. In fact, Bank A has improved on the loan funding profit by 0.106622 per cent, as the exact interest cost for borrowing Cas for one year will amount to 5 per cent—no more, no less—on the 365/365 year basis.

Part of the favourable difference is accounted for by the difference in interest calculation between A and B, *i.e.*

$$\frac{4 \times 365}{360} = 4.05555 \text{ per cent per annum, effective interest.}$$

When converted into the required currency

$$\frac{4.055555 \times 2 \text{ (spot rate)}}{1.98 \text{ (forward rate)}} = 4.096521 \text{ per cent per annum}$$

or simplified

$$\frac{4 \times 365 \times 2}{360 \times 1.98} = 4.096521 \text{ per cent per annum.}$$

Thus most of the favourable result was realized by the difference in interest methods.

By borrowing the Cbs at 4 per cent and thus funding the loan without using the swap market, Bank A would have given up this extra profit, as only the difference between the cost of finance, *i.e.* 4 per cent, and the loan rate would have been converted back into Cas.

Banks do not normally go through all the deposit and foreign exchange transactions to obtain a favourable difference unless the extra gain justifies the extra activity. Dealers should, however, always go through the mechanics of establishing the true interest differential of forward rates by applying the following formulas:

Formula 1

$$\frac{\text{forward margin}}{\text{forward rate}} \times 100 = \text{premium or discount in per cent per annum}$$

Formula 2

$$\frac{\text{rate} \times \text{(days)} \times \text{spot rate}}{\text{(days)} \times \text{forward rate}} = \text{foreign currency interest converted into currency of choice}$$

The days in the formula need to be used only if the year definition differs. By adding premiums or deducting discounts to or from the interest amount, the true yield is obtained.

Difficulties are sometimes encountered with periods shorter than one year, though the formula remains very much the same except that the number of days will have to be added to the set:

Formula 3

$$\frac{\text{premium (or discount)} \times 100 \times 365}{\text{forward rate} \times \text{number of days}} = x \text{ per cent per annum}$$

The number of days can, let us say, be ninety-one for three months, but it must be the exact number of days, not an approximation, and the effective interest rate conversion formula will have to allow for the days only if the interest year definition differs for the two currencies.

Formula 4

$$\frac{\text{rate} \times \text{(days)} \times \text{spot rate}}{\text{(days)} \times \text{forward rate}}$$

For periods in excess of one year the dealer will have to take into account the different interest payments which may take place annually and allow for yearly forward cover of any intervening interest settlements before the repayment of the loan or deposit.

Though he may not engage in it himself, interest arbitrage is a necessary skill for any active forward dealer. Being aware that sure-profit arbitrage situations can be loss-makers and knowing how to calculate effective interest yields will assist him in quoting correct forward rates. In Example 16, the market-maker could not have taken advantage of the discrepancy if the other bank had been aware of the arbitrage situation, which highlights again the importance for forward specialists to be in touch with the deposit markets; otherwise they will be operating in a vacuum.

There are times when arbitrage situations offer the possibility of realizing large profits. These situations will exist only if regulations make it difficult for some parties to take advantage of the fortuitous circumstance; then the case requires careful consideration, not only from a dealing angle. The market mechanism does not offer windfalls under normal conditions.

Technical dates

In some countries money-market activities at a particular time or day of the year can create volatile interest rates, the tendency being for them to go up. For instance, until a few years ago during the first quarter interest rates in the United Kingdom always went up as tax payments came due. This created a shortage of funds in the inter-bank market, and not unnaturally this caused wider discounts for sterling in the forward markets and on rare occasions smaller premiums. In other countries the end or turn of the year and quarter-ends can have the same effect. The local banks and commercial organizations put their house in order or even go in for 'window dressing'. The demand for funds increases in order to show greater liquidity requirements and in direct consequence interest rates for short periods 'skyrocket'.

These technical factors are then reflected in the forward markets for the calendar month(s) within which the technical date(s) falls and the margin will show a distortion. For instance, when forward dollars against Swiss francs are at a discount near a technical date, the forward rates for very short maturities may change to premiums. Skilful dealers anticipate these events and prepare their forward positions well in advance: it is not unusual for operators to take a precautionary position a year ahead in the forward market before the market has adjusted the price structure to allow for any anticipated tightness or easiness.

Forward/forward rates

Because of technical dates, customer requirements for odd-date maturities, or dealers with foresight, there is sometimes a very good market in forward/forward transactions. By 'forward/forward' we understand the simultaneous buying and selling of currencies for maturities further ahead than the spot date. A bank selling dollars against sterling for delivery in three months' time and at the same time buying a similar amount for six months would be engaging in a forward/forward transaction.

Through the market mechanism banks can execute these transactions without appearing to do so. They could, for instance, instruct a broker to buy spot and sell three months forward and at the same time order another broker to sell spot and buy six months, thus leaving a gap between the three and the six months transactions. These transactions can be entered into either to cancel out an existing exposure or to anticipate future developments. If the dealer was reasonably convinced that the forward premium would widen or narrow in three months' time, he might wish to take a *gap exposure* without having to worry about the position from the spot date. Operators tend to look at these forward/forward gaps as something they can forget about until they reach maturity and have to be undone. Naturally they cannot completely forget about their gap exposures, but as long as the forwards do not show a distortion from the existing norm they will not be greatly concerned. If a change occurred before the transaction date, the dealers would very likely take action by dealing from spot until the forward date or even a longer date, thus cancelling out the forward gap and instituting one against spot.

Not many banks deal in forward/forwards on a professional basis, that is to say they do not make special quotations for forward/forward deals, but when they quote forward the contacting party can propose a forward/forward transaction on the rates as indicated, *e.g.* if the three months = 51–49 and the six months = 101–99 the three against six months quotation works out to

$$52 \ (101-49) - 48 \ (99-51).$$

A point that should never be forgotten whether in spot or forward dealing is that when a series of quotations is made simultaneously, and one rate forms the basis for a contract, all the other quotations become void. The quoting bank is then free to make new prices or even to refuse to transact further business at any rate. And, of course, if the contacting bank or customer does not respond 'immediately' to one (or more) prices the market-maker can state that the rates are no longer valid and adjust them without engagement.

Dealing in the professional markets requires immediate reaction to prices, and users who request quotations to be held firm for a limited period of time must appreciate that this service will usually be provided only if the quoting bank can protect itself by quoting less favourable rates.

9. Foreign exchange decisions and commercial organizations

Under fixed-parity systems

Under the Bretton Woods system, or under any other fixed-parity scheme, few definitive foreign exchange decisions had to be made by the participants, as currency translation and transaction losses or profits only had a marginal effect on trading and investment results. With fixed parities, all international organizations have to do is monitor economic data for fundamental imbalances and adopt defensive postures in good time. Usually there will be ample notice as fixed rates obviously tend to move less frequently than floating ones. Under fixed parities the central banks will have to be in the market more often to stabilize the rates, otherwise it would be nonsensical to have a fixed system. Whether hedging or covering operations should be engaged in as soon as a divergence in the figures shows up, or be postponed for as long as seems possible, is a matter of preference, although as hedges are costly they should be entered into only when there are signs that the forward rates are widening and when to postpone the decision will result merely in higher costs. Covering operations, on the other hand, may not be necessary until a currency realignment seems inevitable in the near future. Judgement will have to be exercised as regards the cost of forward cover and the anticipated percentage of the devaluation: if the forward cover cost is greater than the anticipated percentage change after devaluation it may be appropriate to run the exchange risk.

A distinction must be made between 'translation' and 'transaction' losses. The literature on foreign exchange normally assumes that foreign exchange operations for commercial entities always involve some cost, but this is not true at all—there is as much chance for an exchange exposure to turn out profitable as for it to become a loss factor. *Translation results* refer to the impact which a revaluation of foreign currency items will have on the accounts and consequently the balance sheet. *Transaction profit or loss* will refer to the viability of one specific transaction, which will not be separately identified in the balance sheet. There is a tendency for companies to be more concerned with translation than transaction results though the latter may in many cases be more important than the former.

Even in the days of fixed rates some organizations had to be more foreign exchange-conscious than others. For example, commodity houses which handled bulk products with narrow profit margins had to interpret spot and forward exchange trends very carefully because on these small margins depended the end result.

British and United States companies in general tended to be less well versed in foreign exchange techniques than their overseas competitors. This is easily explained by the UK's Commonwealth connections and by the fact that the US dollar was considered to be as good as gold for a long time, and world trade was dominated by both currencies. Competitors in the smaller nations always had to cope with the currency problem; their livelihood depended on it. As world trade was not conducted in their currencies they had to acquire and dispose of the major currencies not only against their own national currencies but also on cross-exchange rates. For a time *Pax Britannica* ruled the political world as well as the international payments system, and even after the First World War British merchants were still protected by the currency linkages within the Commonwealth. With some notable exceptions, in the United States and Great Britain the application of foreign exchange in international pricing remained a forgotten art. US corporations had very little reason to be involved in the currency markets until well after the Second World War and consequently there was limited knowledge of the exchange markets and techniques available.

The situation changed only when the dollar came under suspicion and the gradual dismantling of the British Empire resulted in world trade being based on the dollar instead of sterling.

The expansion of US investment in the 1950s and 1960s was

based on the Bretton Woods system, with the anticipated currency realignments at a maximum of 10 per cent, which, though substantial, would have been compensated by the income flow from abroad. As long as the adjustments were infrequent the income flow would have protected the viability of the investment. In their investment decisions at the time US corporations virtually ignored the currency risk, the emphasis was on profit flows, and the conviction that US management techniques surpassed those of her competitors was, it seemed, unshakeable.

In those heady expansionist days far-reaching investment decisions were made with no concern for the inherent currency risks. Sometimes no thought at all was given to the funding of the operating subsidiary which would be required if the venture proved successful and even more so if it took longer than estimated to become self-financing.

The more astute competition in Europe and the Far East may well have used this lack of expertise in the United States and the United Kingdom to set up pricing and invoicing procedures which eventually could work only to their advantage.

Invoicing in the national currency

Some financial executives fondly imagine that by conducting the international business of their companies totally in the national currency they will escape the impact of currency upheavals. They justify this approach as being conservative, non-speculative and for the good of their organization. Given that some of their foreign suppliers may be in a monopoly position and thus able to dictate price, the currency policy may have to be more flexible in some cases. But this problem can be handled very efficiently; as soon as the invoice is presented forward cover is taken out and the national currency principle effectively applied.

In such a situation import and export prices will have to be compared with those for substitute products in the domestic market, because the treasurer and his assistants will have in most cases little knowledge of the foreign exchange markets. If we refer to Chapter 5 and take another look at the Purchasing Power Parity Theory we will realize that a company which issues and accepts invoices denominated only in the national currency might not be aware of price discrepancies which will from time to time show up. Export prices should, for instance, be compared with prices obtainable in the country of destination. Without applying spot and forward exchange rates, a price struck in the currency of the country of origin may give too much advantage to the foreign importer; while this may be beneficial in that exports will flow out in large quantities, if production has to be increased to meet the demand it may be because the products have been under-priced. If higher prices could have been obtained there might not have been any need to increase production out of proportion. Such an unnecessary increase in production could leave a company with over-capacity when demand slackens because the price or exchange rate differential which favoured exports no longer exists. Export campaigns which use the national currency as a means of pricing should take into account any favourable elements this approach may introduce into the pricing structure. In other words, allowance should always be made for the spot and forward exchange rates, and after taking these into account how the foreign currency price compares with prices in the country of destination.

Whereas the practice of invoicing exports in the national currency can be deplored unless it is based on sound principles, there is an advantage in being invoiced in the national currency for imports. Currency exposure is the concern of the foreign supplier, and as long as the price compares favourably with substitute products not only in the home market but also in that of the country of origin it may even be advisable to use this rate. Companies in weak-currency countries, provided that the necessary precautions are taken to ensure that they do not pay through the nose for the facility, should whenever this is possible request to be invoiced in the national currency. Apart from the avoidance of the currency exposure, it is usually also easier to arrange finance for the import in the national currency.

For every importer there must obviously be an exporter, and what suits one will probably not appeal to the other. If an understanding can be reached by both sides and a price struck which is fair to buyer and seller it would be better for both the parties to the transaction to negotiate a settlement which will benefit them both. As applies to all business transactions, it must be understood that the trading partners do not take advantage of technical aspects such as foreign exchange rates.

To summarize, we could say that for a company to use the national currency only because of conservatism or ignorance is wrong. The national currency can, however, be used if this does not give an unfair advantage to the other party. Nevertheless, knowledge of the foreign exchange market and rate structure, even though it may never be used in practice to transact business, is still a necessity.

Some companies try to circumvent the currency problem by buying from importing specialists, and as the latter invoice in the national currency the company will feel protected from the vagaries of the currency markets. It has been proved on numerous occasions since the middle 1960s that this is a fallacy. By using an intermediary the company may lose control of its import costs and may come to rely on the intermediary more and more. A price escalation may then have to be absorbed without the company having been in a position to take evasive action. Companies using importers in this manner should monitor closely the price structure of the raw materials or components in combination with the foreign exchange rates to ensure that the intermediary is not passing on excessive costs which could have been avoided by exercising greater care in the purchasing of the imports as well as in pricing and foreign exchange cover.

Long-term decisions

International business is becoming steadily more complex. Whereas during the last thirty years the movement has been from the United States towards the rest of the world, this pattern could change. Many internationally active companies now feel that by establishing manufacturing plants in difficult markets advantages can be gained. Of course this will increase the flows of money between countries; marketing and production strategies will be crucial when drawing up long-term investment plans, though less obvious aspects such as whether the currency is strong, what has been the recent history of the exchange rate and how the foreign exchange regulations affect remittance of profits and capital repatriation should also be taken into account. It is better to be prepared for the worst than to be presented with unexpected problems at a later date.

Additional exchange risks associated with foreign-currency invoicing

The one great advantage of using the national currency for both exports and imports is that there is no exchange risk for the importer or exporter. If a foreign supplier fails to deliver the goods or these are unacceptable to the importer, the conservative operator who has bought the necessary foreign currency forward to meet the payment of the invoice may have to cancel out the contract at a loss. The cancellation of the contract may produce a profit as well, but in countries with rigid exchange regulations this may not be looked on in a favourable light by the controlling body since it could be construed that the importer was speculating in foreign currency and that the underlying transaction was a sham.

Similarly, if the currency has been sold forward, the loss may be large should the buyer abroad fail to pay for the goods and the exchange rate moves against the exporter. Again, the exchange transaction could show a profit, in which case the loss would be less.

Fortunately, these days, there are export guarantee schemes in operation in a number of countries and the premium for the service may cover any foreign exchange risks as well. On the whole, it would seem that if the export transaction is a profitable one after allowing for export and exchange cover the premium payable is a small consideration for peace of mind.

Exotic currencies

The exchange problem encountered by merchants who transact business in the major currencies is negligible compared to that incurred by the few traders, usually in commodities, who have to engage in import and export transactions with the under-developed world. With the exception of monopoly situations the currencies used should then not be the indigenous ones but some other hard currency, as there may not be an exchange market in the exotic currency apart from the domestic one. Whether the currency is strong, weak or extremely volatile, the international operator will have no opportunity of fixing the exchange cost if the domestic currency is used.

When entering into a business transaction with a firm domiciled in an unfamiliar country, a careful study should be made of the banking system, the settlement system for international transactions and the delays considered unavoidable. If the domestic currency is to be used, is there a forward market in it and what is the rate structure like?

Conclusion

Whatever precautions are taken, there are circumstances which force financial executives to bear currency exposures for the greater good of their company. As long as these risks are taken after careful analysis of all the facts, the eventual benefits of a new market or source of supply have to be offset against the exchange risk. Naturally the situation should be monitored on a regular basis and when there are opportunities to cover or limit the exposure they should be exploited, as long as the cost of doing so is not prohibitive.

10. Forward exchange and pricing

The importer or exporter who negotiates contracts based solely on spot exchange rates to convert foreign currency prices into the national currency, or the converse, deludes himself. Sadly, many do.

As few transactions involving the movement of goods or services are against immediate, or cash, payment, it is the forward rather than the spot rate which should be applied to judge the competitiveness of a price. The commonest forward rates to be utilized are those for the three and six months maturities, as these are the periods which normally separate the signing of a contract, arrival of the goods and date of payment. Some suppliers will even allow their foreign buyers a period of credit between the arrival of the goods and the payment date. There may be occasions that the importer will receive the proceeds of his sales before payment is due.

The easy way round the exchange rate problem would be to use the national currency at all times for imports and exports, as explained in Chapter 7. And if the price structure takes into account the forward exchange differences, the national currency is always preferable to any other, for the obvious reason that it is the unit of account of the importer's or exporter's country of domicile. This simplistic approach, however, tends to overlook the fact that whatever currency is used to settle an international trade transaction, one of the parties to the deal will have to pay in or receive a foreign currency. If a UK exporter ships goods to Germany and invoices them in sterling, the German importer will have to acquire sterling either in the forward market or at the spot rate when payment is due.

Firms wishing to break into a foreign market may decide to forgo the exchange profits which can be generated, but opportunity losses should be monitored because they could eventually become substantial and in that case the firm's products may well be under-priced.

It would be relatively easy to produce tables of spot and forward rates to prove the point that it would be profitable to use one currency in preference to another, though in reality there are only a few currencies which count in the international payments arena. Some currencies like the Swiss franc may be important for purely financial deals, but for the movement of goods the US dollar, the Deutsche Mark and sterling rank ahead of the others. Naturally, a company trading with France or Japan, or any other country, will have to consider the impact of the French franc or Japanese yen on its prices, and the domestic price structure in these countries, but these transactions do not constitute the bulk of international trade.

How forward rates affect prices can best be illustrated by taking the example of the spot and forward exchange rates for US dollars and Deutsche Marks against sterling, and the US dollar against the Deutsche Mark, as they applied some time during the day on 24th February 1977.

Example 17

| | Against sterling | | Against dollars |
	US $	DM	DM
spot	1.7078–81	4.1025–1125	2.4030–50
three months	1.6748–56	4.0175–0375	2.3990–20
six months	1.6466–74	3.9365–0585	2.3917–47

Instead of quoting the forward margins, the forwards reflect the actual exchange rates for the relevant periods. Rates were volatile during the day but the cross parities are approximately right as a rough and ready conversion shows—DM 4.1075/1.70795 = 2.404930.

A United Kingdom importer with an option to be invoiced in either sterling, dollars or Deutsche Marks based on the spot exchange rates would unhesitatingly have plumped for sterling. Or one would hope so. And if the sterling option was taken away, he would have preferred to be invoiced in dollars rather than Deutsche Marks. The reasons for his decisions are obvious if we look at the effect his preference has on the cost of his import.

The worth of the goods is £1 000 000, or US $1 707 950, or DM 4 107 500, based on the middle of the prevailing exchange rates.

If payment was due in six months' time, the sterling cost would still be the same—£1 000 000—but the dollar and Deutsche Mark costs would have shown a remarkable increase—US $1 707 950/1.6466 (six months' buying rate) = £1 037 258.59 and DM 4 107 500/3.9365 = £1 043 439.60. The extra cost incurred by being invoiced in US dollars would have been bad enough, but to be charged in Deutsche Marks would have gilded the lily for the overseas supplier.

There might be extenuating circumstances which make it propitious to accept invoices in foreign currencies; for instance, if the seller is willing to give credit facilities only subject to the invoice being denominated in a foreign currency. All the buyer will then have to do is to check the forward markets and establish whether the cost of the finance is too high or not compared with the domestic financial alternatives. By having regular contact with the exchange dealers in the banks, and monitoring the current spot and forward rates, it will of course be possible to evaluate the advantage or drawbacks of foreign-currency finance over that domestically available.

Sometimes importers have to live with the fact that suppliers have a monopoly situation. A particular raw material or machine tool is not available elsewhere, but by covering the forward risk they are in a position to establish the real cost of the import and then to pass on the increase in the price of their own products. Although it may be costly, once a risk is covered the importer can spend his time on more positive aspects of his business and try to recoup the loss in other ways.

The foreign exchange and pricing problem is not limited to importers and exporters living in weak-currency countries. The fact that sterling has been demoted to the ranks of the weak currencies has brought the currency dilemma to the fore, but when one day sterling becomes a strong currency once again it will be just as necessary to monitor spot and forward exchange rates. Because then suppliers and buyers abroad may insist on being paid in sterling or prefer to pay in weak currencies.

Example 18

An importer in the United States who would have been presented with the option to be invoiced in Deutsche Marks or in dollars on 24th February 1977 would have been less affected than our importer in the United Kingdom (Example 17). For instance, an import of US $1 000 000 when priced at the Deutsche Mark/dollar spot rate of 2.4040 would have cost DM 2 404 000, and when these Marks were bought forward for six months the effective cost in dollars would have come to DM 2 404 000/ 2.3917 = US $1 005 142.79, thus costing just over half a per cent more than the price expressed in dollars. An insignificant difference, perhaps, but sufficient for a prudent businessman to be concerned about. There is no doubt that the US importer would have responded with alacrity to an offer to be invoiced in sterling based on the spot exchange rate, but it seems highly unlikely that the German supplier would have made the offer in any case.

Both exporters and importers will have to become more expert in foreign exchange in order to be able to check not only the accuracy and appropriateness of prices in other currencies, but also those quoted in their own national currency. It could almost be said that if a supplier or buyer agrees too quickly to a price it must be wrong, and these days the reason for hasty acquiescence may well lie in the forward markets.

Although, in principle, it is rarely wrong to cover any foreign exchange risks in the forward markets, there is one notable exception. If it is almost a foregone conclusion that a currency in which an import is denominated is due to be devalued, or substantially depreciated, it would be wrong to cover in the forward markets unless the forward discount more than compensates for the devaluation percentage that can be realistically expected. If the forward discount is less than the expected percentage adjustment, to cover the exchange risk might well produce an uncompetitive price, particularly if the goods have not as yet been sold. This would particularly apply if the country of origin is in close proximity to that of the importing country and if goods at the old price but in the cheaper currency may be on offer soon after the currency realignment. Naturally, if an import is invoiced in a currency which is revaluation-prone, the forward risk should be covered immediately unless this cost is greater than the anticipated percentage of the revaluation. However, participants in the market should never underestimate the percentages of currency adjustments; in many cases they have been much higher than the experts' predictions.

As a result of the Herstatt and similar débâcles in the foreign exchange market, the banks have been forced to tighten up on foreign exchange procedures and attitudes. The regulatory authorities in the United States and in Europe continue to develop more sophisticated methods of supervising the banks to ensure that they or their dealers do not overtrade or engage in what is euphemistically referred to as 'unauthorized trading'. One of the side effects of the new rules has been that where banks were quite willing to extend a forward contract at the original rate when a customer had mis-timed a receipt or payment, they may now insist on a new rate being fixed for the spot transaction and thus also for the forward prolongation. This means that customers may have to make part-settlements, where previously the two currencies would have matched out on the spot side of the roll-over. The reason for this change in procedure is simply to stop speculation by operators who would not be in a position to fulfil the obligations of a forward contract should the rate(s) move against them. This rule also applies to inter-bank transactions for the same reason.

Up to a few years ago banks—or to put it in perspective, some banks—were more open to the activities of unscrupulous speculators than they are now. All the gambler without a stake would have had to do was to go to a number of banks with a good story and if he found one or more willing to enter into a forward contract with him he could have speculated for fairly large sums, although each bank might only have taken on what they would have thought to be a modest risk to cover a small import or export transaction. Banks are no more or less gullible than private individuals but confidence men who engage in this kind of activity are skilled in their business and will promise that more business will follow if the bank proves its competitiveness in the foreign field. The bank may agree and, let us say, sell sterling against dollars for six months delivery; if at the end of the six months the deal is profitable the speculator will have acquired the reputation of a smart, knowledgeable fellow. On the other hand, if the rate has moved against the speculator he will or could have requested the bank to extend the contract at the old rate, thus ensuring that he would not have to pay the difference; this could have continued until the bank's internal or external auditors spotted the unrealistic rate, but by then, of course, it could be much too late. The speculator might disappear from sight and the bank be left with the exchange loss.

It seems highly likely that transactions of this nature not infrequently took place a few years ago until instructions were given to the banks to use current exchange rates, even for extensions of existing contracts, to stop this fraudulent practice.

For customers, this can mean that if a contract is taken out for six months to convert the proceeds of an export and the shipment is late or the buyers delay payment, to extend the contract may necessitate the customer finding more money, which, if a large amount is involved, could unduly affect his cash flow. While transactions up to one year may not be for large amounts, exports of capital goods payable over several years and denominated in currencies for which there are no forward markets in excess of one year can create problems, particularly if the exporter operates from a country with a weakening currency. Fortunately, in many countries, the problem can be overcome through the intermediary of official or semi-official *credit guarantee bodies*, and with the guarantee of one of these institutions the banks may be willing to provide finance for the shortfall or to continue at the old rate if it can be proved that the underlying transaction is genuine and not speculative.

Option contracts

Option contracts in the foreign exchange market are not like 'put' or 'call' options in stocks or shares, which do not have to be taken up if the stock or share price has not moved in the right direction. Foreign exchange options have to be taken up whether the underlying trade transaction materializes or not. In principle, the shorter the period of the option the better for the party taking out the option. And options are essential only if the effective date of payment cannot be fixed but is likely to take place within a limited span of time. For instance, if an exporter is nearly 100 per cent sure (from past experience) that an overseas buyer will pay within five to six months after shipment (or contract) he can sell the forward currency for delivery to a bank between the five months and the six months date. The five-months date is the first day the option can be exercised, and conversely the six months date is the last day on which the option has either to be taken up, or extended in the case of a genuine trade transaction. By limiting the option to the period between the five and six months date, the seller saves unnecessary expense, as the bank will apply the effective five months rate only if the currency was at a premium, and the six months rate if at a discount; an option from three to six months might have resulted in the bank loading the rate, especially if a change from premium to discount or a narrower premium or vice versa was anticipated.

Example 19

spot rate	Cb	1.9999–2.0001	
three months	Cb	51–	49
five months	Cb	85–	81
six months	Cb	101–	99

If a bank from experience knew that the buyer of a six months option on most occasions took up his option after four months and anticipated no change in this forward structure over the period, it would charge only the five months rather than the six months rate. It might also adopt a similar attitude with a seller: in every instance it will depend on past experience; there are no hard and fast rules.

The professional options market which developed in London during the late 1950s petered out very rapidly. Skilful option-holders were inclined to exercise their options whenever the rates moved in their favour, and only the option-givers incurred losses. All the latter could do was to cease giving options to the regular offenders, and eventually the market died a natural death.

In the United States there have been several attempts to establish genuine 'put' and 'call' options markets in foreign currencies. These are not, however, suitable for commercial interests, as the amounts dealt in are rather small and a margin has to be put up, which on the whole is not necessary when contracting with a bank. These options have furthermore to be taken up on specific days, and few companies could anticipate their settlement requirement dates with that degree of accuracy.

When there is great uncertainty about the future outlook of interest rates and consequently forward margins, the banks quote defensively and the option prices may move away from the fixed market prices. Customers should then query the rate structure but unless they can find another bank with a more optimistic view or more venturesome spirit, they may well be forced to accept the first option rate or take the risk themselves by buying or selling for a fixed maturity. Options serve a particularly useful purpose when a currency is volatile or there is not a very active forward market in it—minor and exotic currencies above all fall within this category.

It is advisable for importers and exporters to monitor the extra costs which they incur not only in interest costs but also in foreign exchange losses when overseas buyers or suppliers do not meet the terms of a contract.

Artificial currencies

Unofficial or official artificial currencies like SDRs have been used in the financial world mainly by government institutions, or very large multi-national companies. For the ordinary commercial user they are definitely not the answer for pricing or exchange exposure problems: the use of them could increase the risks they have to take. Artificial currencies based on a 'basket' of major and minor currencies still require an underlying currency, otherwise payments cannot be made and either the seller or the buyer will be exposed and may not always be in a position to cover the risk in the forward market.

General conclusions

A company which engages only in one-way business—either all imports or all exports—especially when this is conducted with one country alone, is at a disadvantage compared with a company which has in- and outflows in a range of currencies. The latter can apply the use of natural hedges, 'long' of a strong currency, 'short' of a weak one, and thus develop a complete currency exposure strategy. The internationally active company may also be in a position to acquire the services of a foreign exchange expert. In a one-way position, a company should make it its business to monitor the economy and the exchange rate and take action to cover exchange exposure and ensure price-effectiveness whenever this seems appropriate.

Some commercial organizations have hesitated to enter the forward market because they feel that it is a hotbed of speculation. Although this stigma was attached to the forward market a few years ago, even at that time commercial interests dealing with reputable banks would not have suffered. Without using the forward market to cover their currency exposures, or just to facilitate price comparisons, companies would be incurring risks or under-pricing their exports and paying too much for their imports.

11. Exposure management and accounting procedures

It is a fact of life, regrettable perhaps, that the practical foreign exchange dealers and the theoreticians, whether economists or exposure management technicians, rarely see eye to eye. The organic growth of the foreign exchange market has not encouraged the theoretical approach to make the necessary impact. The foreign exchange dealer looks at the market and sees only buyers and sellers, while the exposure manager sees only assets and liabilities and tries to bring them into balance to obviate the need to buy or sell currencies. Exposure management techniques tend to work best in large organizations with large in- and outflows which lend themselves to rational treatment; the middle-sized company is inclined to have special problems which cannot be dealt with in this manner.

A company with exports and imports denominated in many currencies weak and strong may have to take foreign exchange decisions only when a crisis seems imminent; at other times it can take the view that natural hedges exist, although this does not mean that when it comes to pricing forward costs and profit opportunities should be ignored.

Some exposure management methods operate only in inter-group transactions. A Belgian subsidiary exports to Germany and invoices in Deutsche Marks. A French subsidiary imports from Germany and pays in Deutsche Marks. Within the group structure the Deutsche Mark payables and receivables can be netted out and only a Belgian/French franc exchange deal will then be required: one transaction instead of two, saving dealing spreads and possibly running a smaller exchange risk between Belgian and French francs than between Belgian francs and French francs against Deutsche Marks. This kind of *netting out* management also ensures that dealing will take place at the same time, instead of each subsidiary covering its foreign exchange requirements separately. The netting out of all foreign exchange exposures can be handled best by a centre staffed with experts fully conversant with dealing techniques and foreign exchange regulations and in touch with the most competitive banks.

Though exposure management packages can be acquired from, and operated by, specialized banks, few of them will be flexible enough to cover all situations. Basically exposure management should be the responsibility of the commercial organizations and the banks should be called upon only for information or to transact the foreign exchange deal.

To describe every approach to exposure management in detail would be time-consuming and not very instructive, as the efficacy or appropriateness of a method has always to be weighed against a company's flow of funds, corporate organization, tax situation, and whether foreign exchange regulations in a specific country would allow netting out or similar systems.

Multi-national companies which envisage introducing exposure management techniques should consider the flexibility, past performance and information produced by the system and whether it would be more expensive, and more or less effective, than the random decisions of the individual treasurers in the subsidiaries. It may, however, be unfair to judge exposure methods in this way, as by taking away from line managers responsibilities which do not produce greater efficiency or better marketing, the overall result may be that much better.

Whatever the merits or demerits of exposure management for companies with a number of subsidiaries, whether in the same country or abroad, or both, it usually makes sense to set up a separate company to handle all exports, and perhaps imports as well. This company would look after paying and receiving, execute foreign exchange transactions wherever and whenever necessary, finance the operations in the cheapest way possible, advise the other subsidiaries on foreign exchange trends and rates, and perform many other services which cannot be handled adequately by a number of individuals in different locations.

In the absence of a separate export/import company, a specialized division might prove to be just as effective. Companies may find that in order to centralize exposure management and international finance functions they will have to overcome the resistance put up by line managers, who might feel that such centralization will diminish their own status. Organizations which have introduced the concept have, however, proved on the whole that in practice centralization has contributed to the overall efficiency and profitability of all divisions and subsidiaries.

The advent of floating rates has brought in its wake the realization that the older accounting practices are not accurate enough to reflect the greater ups and downs of current exchange rates. Companies which engage simply in exports or imports are not affected to a great extent, but those with subsidiaries abroad may find that the revaluation of overseas assets and liabilities can affect the consolidated balance sheet quite significantly.

The accounting profession is still at sixes and sevens about how to cope with the foreign exchange dilemma, and a satisfactory method which has universal appeal has yet to be invented.

The closing rate method

The commonest way of revaluing foreign assets and liabilities is to convert them at the closing rates prevailing on the last day of the financial year.

Most United Kingdom companies, and many in Europe, apply this system to arrive at the national currency equivalents for consolidation in the parent company's balance sheet. The rates are usually obtained by reference to a suitable daily paper like the *Financial Times* or from the banks if specific rates are not quoted in the press. For some currencies the exchange rates may be purely nominal as there is no effective market in them, or regulations prohibit the repatriation of all assets. Liabilities, for obvious reasons, are rarely affected in this manner. Some organizations in Europe do not consolidate their foreign subsidiaries in their balance sheet, relying solely on the dividend or profit flows to justify the investment. In this case, if the overseas company has an abundance of assets the parent company will under-value its true worth. On the other hand, as the investment for accounting purposes has been written down, its assets and liabil ties are no longer subject to exchange rate fluctuations.

The current/non-current method

This revaluation method distinguishes between short- and long-term assets and liabilities. The first category is revalued at the current or closing rate, whilst the second is evaluated at the *historic rate*, which can be defined as the exchange rate at which an asset or liability was originally created.

The monetary/non-monetary method

The monetary/non-monetary procedure applies current or closing rates to all monetary assets and liabilities, whether short or long term. Non-monetary items such as buildings, inventory, etc., are revalued at the historic rate.

FASB 8

This method, adopted by the Financial Accounting Standards Board in the United States, causes the most concern to US corporations with operating subsidiaries abroad. FASB 8, also called the *temporal method*, uses both closing and historic rates depending on the type of asset or liability. Inventories, for instance, are revalued at the historic rate only if the resultant conversion is lower than if the closing rate had been applied: in other words, inventories are revalued at the worst rate possible. This method is particularly onerous to US institutions which have raised long-term funds in currencies other than those in which their assets are denominated. FASB 8, for all practical purposes, will curtail the borrowings of American corporations in currencies other than those in which they hold assets, or at least have sufficient cash flows to meet interest and capital repayments.

Conclusions

Whatever system of revaluation is used, it cannot represent accurately the true exchange exposure of a company. It is unrealistic to assume, even in accounting terms, that a company would pull out of an operating investment simply because there was a threat of devaluation. Investments are not made on that basis. If a company needs an assembly line or warehousing facilities in another country, this may be essential to its competitiveness in the export markets; a company with a manufacturing subsidiary abroad producing goods for export might find that after a devaluation there is more demand and thus increased profits. In spite of the devalued investment the increased cash flow may then more than compensate for the depreciation of the currency and on a price/earnings ratio the investment may even show an appreciation. Naturally, an investment in a company which sells only into the domestic market of the devalued currencies may not show an increased cash flow, but that is another matter.

Currency exposure managers will have to distinguish between accounting exchange risks and the economic exposure of foreign assets and liabilities, and to produce satisfactory results they may have to combine accounting procedures, economic exposure analyses and foreign exchange techniques in their exposure management. It would be inadvisable to concentrate all efforts on one aspect only, unless the company has no overseas interests apart from imports and exports, in which case they will require only a good knowledge of foreign exchange practices.

12. Forecasting and monitoring foreign exchange rates

It is in fear and trepidation that one mentions 'forecasting' since it seems synonymous with crystal-ball gazing and associated with speculation and gambling. Foreign exchange dealers as well as exposure management exponents will decry a formal forecasting approach as a waste of time and energy. Why this should be is difficult to understand. To say the least, all financial, if not in fact all business, decisions require a degree of risk-taking and forecasting. So why not forecast exchange rates, or at least make an attempt to do so?

If a biscuit manufacturer imported a special ingredient to give his products that extra special taste, he would not be considered a speculator if he covered the exchange risk only at the time of payment. Imprudent, possibly, but he would not be a speculator if he followed the same procedure for every consignment. What would be wrong then if our biscuit king developed an understanding of the economic and financial condition of the country from which he imports the ingredient? And then applies this knowledge in his foreign exchange decisions: 'I'll cover in the forward market because the currency is going to strengthen' or alternatively 'As the currency is bound to weaken I am going to postpone covering the risk.' This would be no different to making a decision to stock up with flour because he feels the price is bound to go up. In other words, a decision about foreign exchange is just another business decision.

Obviously, forecasts can never be 100 per cent accurate. The best one can hope to achieve is to anticipate the direction in which a currency rate will move, but that may well be sufficient for most exchange rate decisions. Some ardent critics of forecasting techniques, and forecasting in general, like to point out that an individual cannot beat the market, but this view is disproved day after day by professional dealers and operators in multi-national companies: they are not out to speculate but to improve their company's performance. Multi-national companies, without a doubt, should apply all the available techniques to increase their earnings and to lessen exposure risks, and forecasting is one of the techniques that should be used. To implement or not to implement techniques or practices should be a deliberate decision which must be subject to revision from time to time.

Anyone wishing to go in for forecasting will have first to evaluate the benefits and the quality of the forecast required, and accordingly calculate the time and manpower that can be allocated to it. One of the first requirements to make possible the construction of a forecasting model is that the exchange rates both for spot and forward transactions are monitored, if not daily then at least once a week. The rates can be obtained from newspapers and friendly dealers, and are also useful in negotiating contracts and thus enabling marketing men and buyers to establish the right prices for imports and exports. Though the forward rates tend to reflect the effective interest rates for a currency most of the time, when the effective interest rates rise or fall more than similar movements in the domestic market this can be an important early indicator of the market's opinion of the currency's future.

With some qualifications, the balance of payments should be the most important input, as the in- and outflows will affect the foreign reserves. Other information which should be evaluated is of course the trade balance, invisibles, inflation levels, money supply and any other fiscal or monetary statistics which could affect the currency's external value or even create a fundamental currency disequilibrium.

Political or social events or changes will also have to be interpreted, as any significant changes may eventually also affect the exchange rate. One does not have to be an expert forecaster to reach the conclusion that constant and substantial balance of payments deficits will necessitate a currency realignment, but, expert or amateur forecaster, the evaluation of non-economic events will be the most difficult aspect of prediction. A sudden change in government is not something that can be anticipated and this may compel the forecaster to revise his view.

Once the executive in charge of the forecasting project has familiarized himself with foreign exchange techniques, economic theory and possibly some mathematical probability studies, he can do some crystal-ball gazing. Initially it may be sufficient to make some very short-term predictions for periods of one to three months. Forecasts for less than one month will rarely be accurate, as short-term factors can influence the exchange rate too greatly. If he finds that his forecast is widely off the mark, but that he judged the trend correctly, he has achieved a worthwhile result. The best any forecast can do is be right about the trend, and if for instance the forecast indicated that covering operations should be postponed and the eventual rate justifies this action the forecasting effort is not wasted.

Several attempts were made a few years ago to use the input of foreign exchange dealers and by averaging all the anticipated exchange rates establish the market consensus as to future exchange rate levels. For example, if the current exchange rate for sterling was 2.40 and on average all the participating dealers expected the rate to be 2.43 in three months' time, and then the spot rate turned out to be 2.41, the forecast was widely off the mark. However, the trend had been interpreted correctly which was at least one positive contribution. Obviously, if a number of exchange dealers in the large banks are of the opinion that an exchange rate is bound to move in one direction their combined actions in the market place may well help to fulfil the prophesy.

In a very simple forecast model, the allocation of numerical values to some of the components can greatly simplify the work of the forecaster. A substantial divergence from the norm set by the forecaster would be sufficient indication to review the input and if this proves to be correct, it may be a warning signal that something is amiss.

The points to look for when studying devaluation- or revaluation-prone currencies are similar, but if a definite tendency has been established it will be necessary to give attention to specific items. For example, for a devaluation-prone currency the relationship between reserves and total imports will have to be monitored. If historically the reserves have covered imports for four or five months a narrowing to two or three months may be the point of no return: the exchange rate will have to be changed. Revaluation-prone currencies may be subject to large inflows of foreign money and as these will affect the money supply, the relationship between the reserves (the increase) and the money supply will have to be watched.

A fair amount of information can be gleaned from the media and political statements. These days a statement by a Minister of Finance that there is no question of a revaluation or devaluation would be all that was needed to stir speculative forces into motion.

Complicated forecasts with a strong mathematical bias are suitable only for very large organizations and may prove to be less effective than simple models as accuracy will depend entirely upon input. It has been said that sophisticated forecasts are very accurate but take so long to put together that the anticipated event has happened before the forecast is complete. A little cynical, perhaps, but not unrealistic as the time, in personnel and computer usage, will make the exercise costly and ultimately not really worth while.

Appendix A. Methodology for theoretical examples

It is customary these days to employ fictional rates in theoretical examples used to illustrate the consequences of foreign exchange decisions and actions since out-of-date exchange rates tend to irritate the knowledgeable reader. Even more important, artificial rates are more suitable for explanatory purposes. In the examples in this book, situations related to past events are based on the exchange rates applicable at the time; the artificial rates used bear some resemblance to the exchange rates for major currencies which have pertained in recent years. Whereas two exchange rates usually suffice for accounting and exposure management models, for our purposes a third currency has had to be invented. For readers versed in the use of market rates, it should be fairly easy to substitute real countries and their exchange rates in place of theoretical quotations.

The countries in the theoretical examples are A, B and C, and their respective currencies Ca, Cb and Cc. Country A follows the indirect quotation system and could thus represent the London market. The following values or exchange rates have been allocated to the currencies of the three countries.

Country A
Currency Ca or Cas
Ca 1 (numeral 1 unit of Currency A) = Cb 2 (2 units of Currency B) = Cc 5 (5 units of Currency C).

Countries B and C adhere to the more common direct quotation system, and their respective exchange rates are valued as follows:

Country B
Currency Cb or Cbs

$$Ca\ 1 = Cb\ 2$$
$$Cc\ 1 = Cb\ 0.40$$

Country C
Currency Cc or Ccs

$$Ca\ 1 = Cc\ 5$$
$$Cb\ 1 = Cc\ 2.50$$

Those conversant with contemporary exchange rates will without hesitation read £1 = US $2.00 for Ca 1 = Cb 2, while Cb 0.40 = Cc 1 and Cc 2.50 = Cb 1 obviously stand respectively for the Deutsche Mark quotation in New York and the dollar quotation in Frankfurt. Ca 1 = Cc 5, by a little stretch of the imagination, could reflect the position of the Deutsche Mark against sterling.

Artificial rates prove invaluable when trying to explain percentage movements from the parity or existing exchange rate. For example, if we assume that the currency of Country B has appreciated by 1 per cent against that of Country A it does not require an advanced degree in mathematics to calculate that the rate of exchange is now Ca 1 = Cb 1.98, as 2.00 divided by 100 equals 0.02. The use of market rates would only complicate matters as a 1 per cent downward change on a rate of 1.7105 would result in a rate of 1.693395, which is not a handy number to utilize in progressions.

Appendix B. Glossary of foreign exchange terminology

Appreciation: Describes a currency strengthening in response to market demand rather than by official action such as revaluation.

Arbitrage: Buying a currency in one centre and selling it in another to take advantage of temporary rate discrepancies. Preferably the two transactions should take place simultaneously, but this is not essential. Arbitrage transactions can take place over many centres and through many currencies before being brought (hopefully) to a satisfactory conclusion.

Arbitrageur: Dealer (trader) who specializes in arbitrage operations.

Banking day: *See* Business day.

Bear: Speculator who sells a currency short in the expectation that a devaluation or depreciation will take place before he has to buy back the currency.

Bear squeeze: Any official action in the market or through regulations which makes it costly or difficult for bears to stay short of a suspect currency.

Best order: Firm order with no rate limit stipulated. Recipient of order is considered trustworthy.

Bid: Normally the rate at which the market in general, or market-maker in particular, is willing to buy a currency. 'Bid', 'pay', 'take' and 'buy' all mean that the quoting or contacting party is interested in buying a currency. Beware, however, when the quotation is a cross-rate for two foreign currencies; then the currency which is of interest should always be specified.

Broker: Intermediary who negotiates foreign exchange deals between banks. In most money centres brokers do not act as intermediary between the banks and commercial users of the market.

Brokerage: Commission charged by a broker for his services. In some countries, this fee is referred to as 'commission'. Brokerage charges can vary depending on currency amount and maturity of the foreign exchange contract.

Bull: Speculator who buys a currency in the hope that it will revalue or appreciate before he has to take delivery and consequently pay for the currency.

Business day: *Also* Banking day, Clear day, Market day and Open day. Day on which foreign exchange contracts can be settled; *e.g.* a foreign exchange contract covering the sale of US dollars against sterling can be finalized only on a day when both New York and London are open for normal banking business (of course, other cities in the US and UK are suitable for payment, but only if they are acceptable to both parties to a transaction).

Buyer's option: Beneficial holder of a buyer's option can take delivery at any time between first day and last day of the option, *e.g.* between spot and a forward date or even between two forward dates, without incurring further costs or for that matter gaining extra profits. *See also* Seller's option.

Buying rate: Rate (*see* Bid) at which the market in general, or a market-maker in particular, is willing to buy a foreign currency.

Cable: Usually refers to the spot dollar/sterling rate.

Clean float: When an exchange rate reflects only normal supply and demand pressures, with little or no official intervention.

Clear day: *See* Business day.

Commercial deal or **transaction:** Foreign exchange deal between a bank and a non-banking party.

Commission: Charges made by a bank to execute a foreign exchange contract with a commercial organization. (In some countries, this charge is made in the exchange rate.) *See also* Brokerage.

Competitive devaluation: Devaluation in excess of estimated equilibrium rate to gain competitive advantage in the export markets.

Confirmation: After transacting a foreign exchange deal over the telephone or telex, the parties to the deal send to each other written confirmations giving full details of the transaction.

Convertible currency: Currency which can be freely exchanged for other currencies or gold without special authorization from the appropriate central bank.

Cover: Foreign exchange deal which protects the value of an import or export transaction against exchange rate fluctuations.

Cross rate: Exchange rate between two foreign currencies, in particular, other currencies against dollars outside the United States. For example, when a dealer in London buys (or sells) Deutsche Marks against US dollars, he uses a cross-rate.

Currency band: Margin within which a currency is allowed to fluctuate by the monetary authorities.

Daylight exposure limit: *See* Intraday position.

Dealer (Trader): Specialist in a bank or commercial company authorized to effect foreign exchange transactions and allowed to take speculative positions.

Depreciation: Currency which loses in value against one or more other currencies, especially if this happens in response to natural supply rather than by an official devaluation.

Details: All the information required to finalize a foreign exchange transaction—name, rate, dates and where payment is to be effected.

Devaluation: Deliberate downward adjustment of a currency in relation to gold or other currencies. A devaluation is necessary only when a currency has fixed parities.

Devaluation-prone currency: Currency which is suspect in the market and which, in the past, has been devalued on a number of occasions.

Direct quotation: Foreign exchange rate which values a foreign currency in terms of the national currency, for example, dollars quoted in Frankfurt in Deutsche Mark terms.

Dirty float: When the value of a floating currency is influenced by the intervention of the central bank.

Discount: Usually refers to the value of a currency in the forward market. When a currency is at a discount compared to the spot rate, it is worth less or, in other words, is cheaper to buy in the forward market than for spot settlement.

End/end: Indicates that both the spot and forward maturity, or two forward maturities in a swap transaction, fall due on the last business day of appropriate calendar months.

Equilibrium rate: Exchange rate at which buyers and sellers are willing to transact business, with supply and demand in balance, possibly only requiring marginal intervention by the monetary authorities.

Euro-currency: Currency held by non-residents and placed on deposit with banks outside the country of the currency. Major Euro-markets exist in Deutsche Marks, Swiss francs, sterling and French francs, and, from time to time, there are active dealings in Dutch guilders, Belgian francs and even Japanese yen. The Euro element is of less importance now that deposit markets have been established in the Far East (the Asian currency market) and in the Western hemisphere.

Euro-dollars: Dollars belonging to non-residents of the US which are invested in the money markets in Europe, particularly in London. Side by side with the Euro-dollar market, there exist the Asian and the Western hemisphere markets. Casual students of the Euro money markets sometimes imagine that there is such a thing as a Euro-dollar note. Of course, this is not the case—Euro-dollar settlements are made over banking accounts in the United States and form an integral part of the US money supply.

Exchange contract: Verbal or written agreement between two parties to deliver one currency in exchange for another for a specific value date, or sometimes a specific period, as in the case of an option contract.

Exotic currencies: Currencies in which there is no active exchange market. Most of the currencies of the under-developed world would fall within this category.

Firm quote (quotation): When a foreign exchange bank gives a firm buying or selling rate, or both, for immediate response or with a definite time limit.

Fixed exchange rate: Official rate set by monetary authorities for one or more currencies. In most instances, even fixed exchange rates are allowed to fluctuate between definite upper and lower intervention points.

Fixing: Exchange rates set in some European countries at specific times of the day, particularly for commercial transactions.

Flexible exchange rates: Exchange rates with a fixed parity against one or more currencies but with frequent up or down valuations.

Floating exchange rate: When the value of a currency is decided by supply and demand only.

Fluctuations: Up and down movements of an exchange rate in response to supply and demand.

Foreign exchange: Conversion of one currency into another.

Foreign exchange market: World-wide network which connects the various national exchange markets by telephone and telex, either direct or via the brokers, to transact foreign exchange business.

Forward book: Various net exposures for forward maturities which a bank has incurred by deliberate policies or as a result of dealing activities.

Forward contract: Exchange agreement between two parties to deliver one currency in exchange for another at a forward or future date.

Forward exchange: Buying or selling currencies for delivery later than spot. Also called 'future'.

Forward/forward: Simultaneously buying and selling the same currency for different maturity dates in the forward market. This also describes a dealer's forward book when he has long and short positions for different maturities, for example, long of Deutsche Marks three months and short of Deutsche Marks in the six months maturity.

Forward margins: Discounts or premiums between the spot rate and the forward rates for a currency.

Forward maturities: Business days for which deals can be transacted later than the spot date.

Forward purchase: Engagement to buy a currency in exchange for another at a future date.

Forward rates: *See* Forward margins.

Forward sale: Agreement to deliver a currency in exchange for another on a future date.

Future: *See* Forward exchange.

Hedging: Act of buying or selling the currency equivalent of a foreign asset or liability in order to protect its value against depreciation (appreciation) or devaluation (revaluation).

Inconvertible currency: Currency which cannot be exchanged for other currencies, either because this is forbidden by the foreign exchange regulations or because there are no buyers who wish to acquire the currency.

Indication (indication rate): When a dealer states 'for indication' or 'indication rate', this means that he does not want to transact business at the given rate or rates. The use of this expression can lead to confusion and it is preferable to substitute the less ambiguous term 'for information only'.

Indirect quotation: Foreign exchange rate which values the local or national currency in terms of the foreign currency. For example, in London foreign exchange rates show the value of £1 in other currency terms.

Interest arbitrage: Switching into another currency by buying spot and selling forward, and investing the proceeds in order to obtain a higher interest yield. Interest arbitrage can be inward, *i.e.* from foreign currency into the local one, or outward, *i.e.* from the local currency to the foreign one. Sometimes better results can be obtained by not selling the forward interest amount, but in that case, if the exchange rate moved against the arbitrageur, the profit on the transaction might be less and even turn into a loss.

Interest parity: One currency is in interest parity with another when the difference in the interest rates is equalized by the forward exchange margins. For instance, if the operative interest rate in the United States is 5 per cent and in the United Kingdom 6 per cent, a forward premium of 1 per cent for US dollars against sterling would bring about interest parity.

Intervention: When central banks operate in the exchange markets to stabilize the rates and sometimes to influence the external value of a currency.

Intraday position: Overall foreign exchange exposure in one or more currencies a dealer is allowed to run during the dealing day for limited periods. *See also* Overnight limit.

Leads and lags: Process of accelerating or delaying foreign exchange cover when a currency adjustment seems imminent.

Limit order: When a buy or sell order is placed at a specific rate or better. *See also* Stop-loss order.

Limited convertibility: When residents of a country are prohibited from buying other currencies even though non-residents may be completely free to buy or sell the national currency.

Long position (or just **Long):** Incurred when a dealer purchases a currency in excess of his immediate requirements. Obviously a long position in one currency is compensated by a short position in another, even if the other currency is the national one.

Managed float: When the monetary authorities intervene regularly in the market to stabilize the rates or to aim the exchange rate in a required direction.

Margin (Spread): Difference between the buying and selling rates, but also used to indicate the discounts or premiums between spot and forward.

Market day: *See* Business day.

Market-maker: Bank which makes buying and selling quotations in one or more currencies, either for spot and/or forward, to most comers.

Maturity date: Due date of an exchange contract, that is, the day that settlement between the contracting parties will have to be effected.

Mine: Expression sometimes used to indicate that the contacting party is willing to buy at the rate offered by the quoting bank. As the term can lead to misunderstandings, it is better to use 'I buy' or 'I take' rather than 'Mine'.

Odd dates: Non-standard days in the forward market.

One-way market: Market where participants are either only buyers or only sellers.

Open day: *See* Business day.

Options: *See* Buyer's Option and Seller's option.

Outright: Simple foreign exchange transaction involving either the purchase or the sale of a currency.

Overnight limit: Net long or short position in one or more currencies that a dealer can carry over into the next dealing day.

Over-valuation: Describes the exchange rate of a currency which is in excess of its purchasing power parity. This means that the country's goods will be uncompetitive in the export markets.

Package deal: When a number of exchange and/or deposit orders have to be fulfilled simultaneously.

Pip: The fifth place after the decimal point, for example $/£: 1.72105. The last digit represents five pips.

Point: The fourth place after the decimal point is called a 'point', for example $/DM: 2.4010. The last digit (0) represents zero points.

Premium: A currency is at a premium, especially in the forward market, when fewer units can be bought for a forward maturity than on the spot. *See also* Discount.

Revaluation: When the official value of a currency is up-rated by a deliberate decision of the monetary authorities.

Roll-over: Prolongation of a maturing contract by swapping it into a forward date.

Seller's option: Forward contract which allows the seller to deliver the foreign currency on any date within the option period. *See also* Buyer's Option.

Selling rate: Rate at which a market-maker will sell a foreign currency for a suitable maturity date.

Short forward date and **rate:** The term 'short forward' can refer to periods up to two months, although it tends to be used more and more for maturities of less than one month. Dealers may use the term 'Shorts' as well.

Short position: When a dealer is short outright of a foreign currency. *See also* Long Position.

Speculator and **speculation:** Individual, and act of buying and selling a currency, in the hope that, before the currency has to be paid for or delivered, a favourable exchange rate adjustment will take place.

Spot: Generally the spot date falls two business days after the transaction date, though in some markets spot transactions may be executed for value next day.

Spot deal (transaction): Foreign currency purchase or sale effected for spot value.

Spot rate (Exchange rate): The spot rate is also the exchange rate of a currency and is the one against which appreciations and depreciations (devaluations and revaluations) will be calculated.

Square: Purchases and sales are in balance and thus the dealer has no position.

Stop-loss order: Order given to ensure that, should a currency weaken by a certain percentage, a short position will be covered even though this involves taking a loss. 'Realise Profit Orders' are less common.

Spread: *See* Margin (spread).

Support levels: When an exchange rate depreciates or appreciates to a level where the monetary authorities usually intervene to stop any further up or downward movement.

Swap: Transaction involving the simultaneous buying and selling of a currency for different maturities.

Swap margin: *See* Forward margin.

Swap rate: *See* Forward margin.

Thin market: When there is little activity in the market and even small orders will affect the rate structure.

Today/Tomorrow (also **Overnight**): Simultaneous buying and selling of a foreign currency for value same day against the next, or vice versa.

Tomorrow next (Tom next): Simultaneous buying of a currency for delivery the following day and selling for the spot day, or vice versa.

Transaction date: Day on which a foreign exchange transaction is entered into.

Transaction loss (or profit): Real or opportunity loss or profit on a foreign exchange transaction covering the movement of goods or services or even to undo another foreign exchange transaction.

Translation loss (or profit): Estimated loss or profit resulting from the revaluation of foreign assets and liabilities for balance sheet purposes.

Two-way quotation: When a dealer quotes both buying and selling rates for foreign exchange transactions.

(Order) Under reference: Before finalizing a transaction all the details should be submitted for approval to the order-giver, who has the right to turn down the proposal.

Under-valuation: An exchange rate is under-valued when it is below its purchasing power parity. The consequence of under-valuation is that the goods produced in the under-valued country will be too cheap in the export markets.

Valeur compensée (Compensated value, also **Here and there):** Principle which governs foreign exchange transactions, that on the due date the payment from both parties will be effected simultaneously in the two centres. In practice, this is an impossibility as, for instance, the New York banks open for business approximately at the time that the European banks close their doors. Consequently, there will always be a time lag.

Value date: Maturity date of a spot or forward contract.

Value today: Transactions executed for same-day settlement; sometimes also referred to as 'cash transactions'.

Value tomorrow: Transactions effected for settlement the next day.

Appendix C. Bibliography

AMERICAN BANKERS' ASSOCIATION: *Foreign Exchange Trading Techniques and Controls*, 1976.

CRUMP, Norman: *The ABC of the Foreign Exchanges*, Macmillan, London, 1963.

EINZIG, Paul: *A Dynamic Theory of Forward Exchange*, Macmillan, London, 1975.

EINZIG, Paul: *A Textbook of Foreign Exchange*, Macmillan, London, 1973.

EINZIG, Paul: *A History of Foreign Exchange*, Macmillan, London, 1963.

EINZIG, Paul: *Foreign Exchange Crises*, Macmillan, London, 1968.

EINZIG, Paul: *Leads and Lags*, Macmillan, London, 1968.

EINZIG, Paul: *The Case Against Floating Exchanges*, Macmillan, London, 1970.

EVITT, H. E.: *A Manual of Foreign Exchanges*, Pitman, London, 1971.

HOLGATE, H. C. F.: *Exchange Arithmetic*, Macmillan, London, 1973.

HOLMES, Alan, and SCHOLT, Francis H.: *The New York Foreign Exchange Market*, New York Federal Reserve Bank, 1965.

PRINDL, A. R.: *Foreign Exchange Risk*, John Wiley & Sons, New York and London, 1976.

Swiss Bank Corporation: *Foreign Exchange*, 1973.

Wainman, David: *Currency Fluctuation: Accounting and Taxation Implications*, Woodhead-Faulkner, Cambridge, 1976.

Weisweiller, Rudi: *Foreign Exchange*, George Allen & Unwin, London, 1972.

Index